SURVIVING
Tenko

D1353430

SURVIVING
tenko

THE STORY OF
MARGOT TURNER

PENNY STARNS

First published 2010

The History Press
The Mill, Brimscombe Port
Stroud, Gloucestershire, GL5 2QG
www.thehistorypress.co.uk

British Library Cataloguing in Publication Data.
A catalogue record for this book is available from the British Library.

ISBN 978 0 7524 5553 2

Typesetting and origination by The History Press
Printed in Great Britain
Manufacturing managed by Jellyfish Print Solutions Ltd

This book is dedicated with love to my father,
Edward A. Starns

Contents

Acknowledgements

The process of writing this book has been greatly assisted by military personnel who generously helped me during the research for my PhD thesis into nursing history. They gave me their time along with valuable insights into the field and history of military nursing; they include Colonel Gruber Von Arni, RRC, Major Jane Titley (retired 1995), Major McCombe and the late Dr Monica Baly. In addition, I am grateful to a number of archivists, particularly Elizabeth Boardman, Jonathan Evans and Susan McGann, who assisted this extensive research process.

I would like to take this opportunity to thank my friends Joanna Denman, Derrick Shaw, Charlotte and David Hodes, the late Brenda Wood, Jo Foster and Cathy Nile for listening to my ideas as always, and for their practical support. I extend a heartfelt thank you to my father who first encouraged my love of history and has patiently supported my quest for knowledge. I am also indebted to my editor Sophie Bradshaw and Abbie Wood at The History Press for their patience and guidance. Special thanks are due to my three sons Lewis, Michael and James for keeping me on track while I wrote this biography and to my brother Christopher for his encouragement. In addition, I am grateful to all those military nurses past and present who have helpfully recounted their experiences in the field of combat in order to provide the context for Dame Margot's story. Please note that all memorabilia relating to Dame Margot, including the powder compact with which she collected her precious rainwater whilst adrift on her raft, is held at the Queen Alexandra's Royal Army Nursing Corps Museum, the Royal Pavilion, Aldershot.

Sources

The main primary source material for this biography has been supplied by the Imperial War Museum in the form of Dame Margot Turner's oral history interviews. Additional primary source material was obtained from The National Archives, mainly War Office Records, Medical History Records, Ministry of Health Records and General Nursing Council Records. Some contemporary newspaper articles have also been consulted. Secondary material includes an earlier biography of Dame Margot that was written by Sir John Smyth, entitled *The Will to Live*, and published in 1970; and an account of the experiences of women interned in Japanese prisoner-of-war camps written by Lavinia Warner and John Sandilands, entitled *Women Behind the Wire*, which was published in 1982.

All the royalties resulting from this book will be donated to the charity Help for Heroes.

Introduction

Much of the literature concerning women and the Second World War has focused on the European conflict. With this emphasis on European battles and victories there has often been a tendency to overlook the brave and resilient women who were captured and interned in the Far East. Yet these women were truly remarkable in their own imitable ways. They established all-female societies within the confines of Japanese prisoner-of-war camps and ran these societies along the lines of liberal democracies, despite the tyranny of their overseers and the deprivations of their captivity. This book charts the life of one of these courageous women, an outstanding military nurse named Dame Margot Turner. Before summarising her experiences, however, it is perhaps pertinent to briefly outline the history of military nursing and its role as a vocational profession with noble and honourable roots.

For much of the nineteenth century British nursing lacked a clear professional identity. The sick were cared for more often by relatives and friends than by individuals in possession of recognisable nursing skills. Additional care was provided when necessary by religious sisterhoods and domestic handywomen. Military nursing was predominantly a male domain as women were considered to be too delicate to care for severely injured men. During the Crimean War the War Office did permit a party of female nurses, led by Florence Nightingale, to nurse the troops in Scutari. This move was viewed as an experiment and, despite the myths that have surrounded the Nightingale legend, the War Office did not fully endorse a commitment to female nursing until after the Boer War. Nightingale had, however, provided the initial breakthrough necessary for the formation and expansion of a female military nursing service. She had also established a more humane and hygienic system of care for wounded soldiers. Upon her arrival in Scutari the hospital was overflowing with sick and wounded men. Some of the men had previously been onboard ships for over three weeks with little in the way of care and minimal rations. Once they became hospital patients many were left to lie aimlessly in soiled uniforms and bandages:

> Hell yawned. Want, neglect, confusion, misery … filled endless corridors … The very building itself was radically defective. Huge sewers underlay it, and cesspools loaded with filth wafted their poison into the upper rooms; here there was no ventilation. The stench was indescribable. There were no basins, no towels, no soap, no brooms, no mops, no trays, no plates, stretchers, splints, bandages – all were lacking.[1]

Nightingale quickly organised her nurses into an efficient team and laboriously scrubbed and cleaned every inch of the Scutari Hospital. Undoubtedly she was the beloved, gentle lady with the lamp to her wounded soldiers, but she was simultaneously a formidable tour de force on their behalf. Reams of letters poured out from the hospital directed to the British War Office, penned by Nightingale herself, which detailed the desperate medical situation and the scandalous shortages of basic hospital supplies. More importantly, Nightingale knew exactly how to get her own way, and threatened to inform the press if supplies for her soldiers were not forthcoming. In addition to setting up a clean and hospitable environment for the wounded men, she established a reading room for their convalescence and a method by which they could send a portion of their wages back home to their wives and families. Not content with merely reorganising the hospital and improving the lives of the sick and wounded, Nightingale also compiled medical statistics, and later assisted Henri Dunnant with the founding and organisation of his international Red Cross movement.

Following the Crimean War a grateful British public donated sums of money and established the Nightingale Fund. Money from this fund was used to create the first secular nurse training schools to be based on Nightingale's principles. Thus, in 1860 a military nurse training school was founded at Netley and a civilian nurse training school at St Thomas' Hospital. In order to comply with Victorian conventions Nightingale established dormitory style homes for probationer and trained nurses and insisted that their characters were rigorously evaluated before they entered training schools. It was important for all nurses to avoid any whiff of scandal and to conduct themselves in a ladylike manner.

Military values were incorporated into both military and civilian training schools and these revolved around a sense of duty, self-sacrifice, discipline and respect for authority. Nightingale likened the effects of military nursing to that of a pebble thrown into water; the ripple effect of kindness, nurturing and servitude to the wounded soldier assisted his recovery and instilled him with memories of a dignified nursing service. The process also reminded the soldiers of their wives, girlfriends, sisters and mothers back home, and boosted their morale as they recalled their homes and hearth. She often compared the military nurse with the soldier in terms of the discipline that was required by both. Discipline, she argued, was what made people 'endure to the end'. Training in obedience was essential to make sure that 'every person did their own duty rather than every man going their own way'.[2]

By the turn of the century the Nightingale nurse training system had been adopted across the country, and as Britain prepared for the First World War military nursing became a vital component in the drive towards nurse registration and the female suffrage movement. As Dr Summers has argued: 'It was thought that women's necessary services in war demonstrated their de facto equality with men and their right to franchise.'[3]

The Representation of the People's Act in 1918 gave limited voting rights to women and by 1919 nurses had won their thirty-year battle for nurse registration and government recognition. However, the Nightingale system had ossified in the civilian field, and left little room for improvements in working conditions and nursing practice. Military nursing, in contrast, had adapted to modernity, and maintained its emphasis on leadership and war preparation in terms of medical and health care delivery. Military nursing was considered to be the elite field of nursing, a profession founded on strong principles and military value systems. Therefore, while many civilian hospitals struggled to recruit young girls for nurse training, once their training and registration was completed, the military nursing field had no problem whatsoever in attracting these girls into their ranks. As one of the later military nurse recruitment pamphlets pointed out:

> You will work in up to date hospitals with modern equipment nursing service women as well as soldiers, their wives and children, and civilians. Your career in the QAs will normally bring a fresh posting every two years, perhaps to Hong Kong, Nepal, West Germany, Cyprus, Northern Ireland ... wherever you go, you may have the opportunity to use any specialist qualifications you may possess, and plenty of time to be a good nurse. And except in the rare emergency you will never find yourself with too many patients. Off duty: Comfortable accommodation is provided for everybody ... you are well looked after in the modern army. You can join in with other serving men and women in dramatic and folk singing clubs. Your social life – in effect – can be as active and varied as you like.[4]

The prospect of nursing with the elite, rendering a patriotic and vital service to their country, travelling across the world and being relieved of the normal domestic expectations of womanhood, were all cited by girls as reasons for entering the military nursing service. Throughout the Crimean War, Boer War and the First World War, British military nurses became renowned for their commitment to their country, their sense of dignity and duty, and their self-sacrifice. In addition to their founder Florence Nightingale, the nursing profession became littered with the names of extremely brave women such as Edith Cavell. Viewed in this historical context, therefore, the extraordinary life of Dame Margot Turner clearly followed a finely carved path of heroic nursing tradition.

Among the memoirs of women who served during the Second World War, those of Dame Margot Turner stand out like a beacon of light. Indeed, her experiences were so unusual and dramatic that they prompted the highly successful 1970s television series *Tenko*. Dame Margot was working as a theatre sister with the QAIMNS (Queen Alexandra's Imperial Military Nursing Service) in Singapore at the time of its surprise capitulation in February 1942. British and Indian troops were quickly evacuated. Along with about 350 others, Dame Margot boarded a cargo ship in Keppel harbour in an attempt to escape the invading Japanese forces. This ship was subsequently shelled and its mixed cargo of military personnel and civilians were tossed unceremoniously into the sea. After swimming to a nearby island, a few days later Dame Margot boarded another cargo ship bound for Batavia; this was torpedoed and once again she found herself fighting for her life.

Surrounded by shark-infested waters and struggling to keep on top of the strong, dangerous currents, Margot and another QA managed to construct a makeshift raft. One by one, however, the others on the raft, including a small baby, died. They perished as a result of their wounds, heat exposure and dehydration. Burnt black, and blistered by the fierce Asian sun, Dame Margot survived on her raft by eating seaweed and drinking rainwater that she had collected in her powder compact. Eventually she was discovered by a Japanese destroyer and its crew mistakenly believed her to be Malayan because of her black skin. When the true nature of her nationality was revealed she was initially interned on the small island of Banka, near Sumatra.

For the next three and a half years Dame Margot lived and worked in Japanese prisoner-of-war camps, even enduring a spell in the notorious Palembang prison with murderers and thieves. Her experiences were often horrific, but occasionally heart-warming and surprising. The following pages tell the dramatic story of how she survived her shipwreck ordeals and internment at the hands of the Japanese to become a brigadier and the matron-in-chief and director of the Queen Alexandra's Royal Army Nursing Corps.

Notes

1. L. Strachey, *Florence Nightingale* (1997), pp. 16–7.
2. M. Baly, *As Miss Nightingale Said* (1991), p. 91.
3. A. Summers, *Angels and Citizens* (1988), p. 182.
4. Ministry of Defence Recruitment Pamphlet (HMSO), 1981.

I

The Young Margot

I t was somewhat ironic, given her later association with the Japanese, that Margot Evelyn Marguerite Turner was born on 10 May 1910 in Finchley a mere four days before the grand opening of a major Japanese exhibition in the White City area of London. Designed to underpin the renewal of an Anglo–Japanese alliance, the exhibition occupied 242,700 square feet and included nearly 300 exhibitors. Furthermore, it was an unprecedented and ostentatious display of Japanese culture that generally portrayed Japan as a progressive and modernising nation with a complementary empire. To the chagrin of the Japanese government, a few exhibitors chose to highlight the poverty and plight of the peasant population and showed examples of officially sanctioned barbaric behaviour; but overall, visitors were impressed by images of Japanese gardens, exquisite silk kimonos and Far Eastern prosperity. The exhibition ran until 29 October 1910 and received favourable and polite reviews in the British press. Although some more patriotic journalists smugly pointed out that while Japan's Empire of the Sun was indeed enviable, the sun never went down on the British Empire.

The year of Margot's birth was eventful for reasons other than the major Japanese exhibition. It was the year that marked the death of King

Edward VII, Florence Nightingale and Leo Tolstoy. It was also the year that Sir George White began his highly successful aircraft manufacturing business in Filton, Bristol. There was a violent upsurge in the women's suffrage movement and the Liberals swept to victory in the December general election. Increasing international tension had prompted health and welfare initiatives to improve potential recruits to the armed forces and Britain was involved in an expensive naval arms race with the kaiser's Germany. This volatile situation had created a distinctly jingoistic and militaristic Britain, which hurtled unstintingly towards the First World War.

In Margot's local area of Finchley, political and world events were temporarily usurped in 1910 by the grand opening of the East Finchley Picturedrome. Now a grade two listed building it was also known as the Phoenix cinema, and was one of the first to introduce sound pictures in 1929. Margot's family were of quiet middle-class origin, and her mother Molly Cecilia and father Thomas Frederick Turner, a solicitor's clerk, were already the proud parents of two sons, Dudley and Trevor, before Margot appeared on the scene. A younger brother named Peter arrived soon afterwards, and it was not surprising, given all this brotherly influence, that Margot became renowned as a 'tomboy' type during her youth.

Physically, Margot was as strong as an ox and revelled in sports of all kinds. In her adolescence she particularly excelled in swimming, hockey and tennis. By this time she was well-built, tall and with a handsome rather than a pretty face. Friends of the family constantly remarked on her twinkling pale-blue eyes, good bone structure and dishevelled light-brown wavy hair. They described her face as one that expressed a certain degree of kindness combined with a mischievous, wry sense of humour. Taller than most of her peers by the time she was 15, Margot was an imposing figure with an understated natural air of authority.

Britain during the interwar years was dogged by industrial strife and economic depression. Six national hunger marches began in 1922 and long-term unemployment was an increasingly worrying problem for over a million families. The National Strike in 1926 was a turning point in labour relations and the Prime Minister Stanley Baldwin took a firm stance against the miners and their supporters by bringing in the troops to settle the matter. There continued to be fluctuations in unemployment figures, however, and the north/south divide was apparent, with the latter being more affluent and able to ride the economic downturns.

The economy did not fare much better in the 1930s but at least some improvement was in sight. Nevertheless, just as the economy seemed to be on the mend, the country was rocked by another problem that shocked the nation. On 20 January 1936 King George died and his son became King Edward VIII; a few months later it was obvious that the latter had embarked on an affair with double divorcee Wallis Simpson. A determined Stanley Baldwin dealt with the subsequent abdication crisis in a forthright and relatively swift manner. Thus, by 8 December 1936, the king had made up his mind to give up the throne for the woman he loved. His brother, therefore, became King George VI. But the country was divided for a long time afterwards, with over 60 per cent of the British population expressing some sympathy towards the abdication dilemma faced by King Edward VIII. This did not mean that they were averse to the new King George VI. Indeed, the quiet, dignified manner of the latter endeared him to a good many people, and his wife Queen Elizabeth proved to be an astonishing and much-loved asset to the throne.

The interwar political events in Britain were turbulent and unpredictable. Many of them were overlooked by the young Margot, however, who was more interested in sport and animals than politics at this stage. Whenever she was asked about her early years Margot always maintained that her childhood was very happy and totally uneventful. But there was no doubt that she had succeeded in suppressing a number of distressing emotions. Her father died when she was only 13 and she had wrestled with this grief in a very private way. Margot did not believe in airing her feelings to all and sundry, and stoically mourned her father in a peculiarly insular way. She studiously read the Bible, hoping to gain some divine perspective on the issues of life and death, and immersed herself in long periods of quiet introspection and prayer. She also spent time comforting her mother and brothers and discussed her deep religious faith with them at length. Margot was a very popular girl and her classmates at Finchley County School described her as forthright, honest, loyal, compassionate and dedicated. She was also practical, thoughtful and self-disciplined. Eventually her mother acquired a second husband, a gentleman named Ralph Saw, who

Margot readily accepted as her stepfather and later described as a perfectly charming man.

It was around this time that the family moved to Hampstead and the teenage Margot began to think about her future career path. Being an outdoor, adventurous girl, Margot could not bring herself to contemplate a career that might confine her to an office. Moreover, it seems that a number of influences and experiences guided her, almost by stealth, into the nursing profession. The large volume of men who had returned from the First World War physically dismembered and mentally crippled had ignited her sympathy and compassion. From the age of 8, like everyone else in Britain, she was surrounded by people who had been affected either directly or indirectly by the tragic conflict. The influenza pandemic of 1918 had also left an indelible impression on the young Margot.

Since, in the days before vaccines and antibiotics, many victims only survived because of the timely intervention of good nursing care, it became clear to the practical Margot that nursing was not only a useful profession but one that could make a real difference in terms of serving humanity. Furthermore, the profession appealed to her religious sensitivities. Some of her older school friends had already embarked on a nursing career and a chance meeting with these girls in 1930 clarified her thoughts. Consequently, Margot began her nurse training at St Bartholomew's Hospital in London the following year.

St Bartholomew's was affectionately known as Bart's by all its doctors and nurses. The hospital was originally established in 1123 by a favoured royal courtier named Raherus. While on a pilgrimage to Rome, Raherus fell seriously ill. In a feverish state he had prayed for recovery, vowing to God that he would build a hospital for the 'recreacion of poure men' should his wish be granted. He was rewarded with a vision of St Bartholomew and the saint instructed him to build a hospital with a priory attached. Raherus duly obliged and St Bartholomew's became one of London's finest hospitals. By the time Margot began her nurse training in 1931 Bart's had an enviable reputation and belonged to a group of highly esteemed London hospitals that operated within the voluntary hospital sector.[1]

With its traditional reputation for excellence, Bart's could afford to operate elitist recruitment practices and all job interviews were painstakingly gruelling. Each year nearly 50 per cent of girls who were interviewed for a nurse training place were rejected out of hand. The others needed to be approved by the discerning matron Miss Helen Day and, as probationers, would begin a six-week course at the preliminary training school in Goswell Road.

The probationer drop-out rate at the end of the six-week period was often much more than 50 per cent, though in Margot's cohort twenty probationers began the training and ten of these had left before the end of the preliminary course. After this training period, the remaining probationers began working on the wards at Bart's for a trial period of three months. A final selection process was then conducted by Matron and the hospital governor in an imposing interview room with two adjacent doors. Selected probationers left the room by one door and rejected probationers by the other. Given the high rejection rate Margot was greatly relieved when she passed this final selection interview. Once accepted onto the four-year training course, she moved into the lively nurses' home, which housed around 520 nurses, and settled into her new career with enthusiasm.

Nurse training at this point in time was not for the faint-hearted. The hours of work were extremely long and it was not unusual for a probationer to work at least seventy-two hours a week, sometimes only having one day off a month. In addition to the daily grind of ward work, probationers also needed to study in their off-duty hours in order to pass their examinations. Rates of pay were poor, but the young girls were at least provided with safe accommodation and meals. They had very little time for a private or social life and were rigidly supervised by a home sister and Matron. Furthermore, any probationer who met a man and chose to marry was forced to instantly resign from the profession, since nursing was considered to be a vocation that required total dedication.[2]

A typical day for Margot began at 6 a.m. with a wash and breakfast. Ready for duty and on the ward by 6.30 a.m., she would then check all the patients' temperatures, blood pressures and pulses before administering their tea and breakfasts. Bed-making, washes and bed baths, operating theatre preparations and dressing wounds kept the probationers occupied for most of the morning. Senior probationers would accompany trained nurses on their medicine rounds in order to learn the correct dosage and administration methods of individual drugs. The more junior probationers were expected to clean the bedpans, vomit and sputum bowls, and the shelves and walls of the sluice. During the patients' visiting hours they would clean cupboards, roll bandages and wash and prepare the stainless steel instruments for sterilisation. Hot kaolin poultices were prepared each day to draw out the infection from abscesses and septic skin areas, and frothy mixtures of egg white were whisked and placed on bed sores and exposed ulcers to aid healing. Despite their early morning start, probationers did not complete their day shift until 8 p.m. There was just enough time for them to eat supper, drink cocoa and retire to bed.

Life in the nurses' home was governed by a specially designated home sister and a list of strict rules about behaviour. Notices were posted on just about every wall, with instructions on how to keep the kitchen and utensils clean and the bathroom spotless. Probationers were instructed to ration their hot bath water, on the grounds that others would also need to use the supply and the fact that having a bath which was too hot lowered the vitality of the nurse and reduced their resistance to infection. There were also amusing notices designed to reduce electricity consumption, like the instruction to young probationers to eat bread rather than make toast, because bread was better for them and more nourishing than toast!

Each individual room in the nurses' home contained very basic furniture: an iron bedstead and lumpy mattress, an old battered-looking wardrobe, a freestanding black, iron-framed mirror and a bedside table. A long list of rules was posted on the inside of every door and nurses were usually informed that they needed to turn their mattress over before making their bed and attending breakfast, and to open the windows whatever the weather in order to air their rooms. All suitcases were usually labelled and kept in a separate room to prevent some of the more homesick probationer nurses from running away in the middle of the night.

The need to conform to a seemingly endless set of rules and regulations deterred most girls from entering the nursing profession, but these strict practical codes were accompanied by another set of rules which governed behavioural and personality traits. According to these, probationers needed to conform to specific and rather angelic characteristics. Official guidelines produced by nursing magazines stated that a nurse probationer needed to be intelligent, possess cleanly habits, a perfect temperament, good physical stamina, natural obedience, an ability to accept discipline, mental and emotional stability, and smart appearance. Indoor and outdoor uniforms were provided by the hospital, and when off duty nurses were expected to wear clothes that stressed modesty and prevented any possibility of provoking excitement in the opposite sex. A nurse also had a duty to take care of herself, as one article explained:

> Passing her life amid scenes of sorrow, suffering and the results of what she has been taught to consider sin, she tends to become morbid, introspective and cramped. She must, therefore, off duty, seize every chance of relaxation in any sphere unconnected with her work.[3]

Matrons and nursing home sisters were trained to watch out for signs of melancholia and other character defects in their probationers, but despite their concerted and occasionally misguided efforts, a large number of probationers did not continue their nurse training past the first year. Homesickness was a huge problem for a lot of young girls, and the unfamiliar hospital territory was daunting for many. Monica Dickens recalled her early days as a young probationer as follows:

> For the first few days I groped my way through a dust storm of new impressions, baffling orders and mystic phraseology, but gradually the dust began to settle into the pattern of hospital life. What had seemed like chaos at first emerged as a routine so rigid that it superseded any eventuality. The ward work must go on. That locker must be polished without and scoured within, though death and tragedy lie in beds on either side. Soon I could hardly imagine a time when I had not done exactly the same things at the same time each day. I sometimes caught myself thinking how deadly the work would be if it were not for the patients, forgetting that without patients there would be no work, for it seemed to have an independent existence, which nothing could ever stop.
>
> If all the beds were empty one would still come on at seven o'clock and push them backwards and forwards and kick the wheels straight.

As it was, life became more bearable with each day's knowledge of the patients and the realisation that they were people, not just bodies under counterpanes whose corners had to be geometrical. Of course, there was hardly any time to talk to them, but sometimes, closeted behind screens to give a blanket bath, you could get down to a good gossip, until a long white hand drew back the screen to admit the ivory face with its fluted nostrils and fastidious lips. 'Neu-rse' – Sister Lewis's voice had a kind of disdainful creak – 'you're giving a blanket bath, not paying a social call.' She was on speaking terms with me by now, or at least on telling-off terms. I was responsible for an unmentionable little apartment called the sluice, which she would enter every morning at nine o'clock, almost changing into old shoes to do so. She would sniff delicately and touch things with her fingertips, but her eye was ruthless. There was usually something that had to be cleaned again and I would have to miss part of the half hour's break we were allowed for making our beds, changing our apron and having a cup of coffee.

If I had been surprised by the capacity of the nurses' stomachs at breakfast, I was staggered when I did get time to go to the dining room for what was known as lunch. The ends of yesterday's long loaves were on the table, with a mound of margarine and a bowl of dripping. I tasted the dripping once, and tasted it all day in consequence. The next meal was called dinner. This was served at midday, except for the senior nurses, and there were all the white pigeons again, ready to make up for only two slices of meat by quantities of potatoes and as many goes of rice pudding they could manage before sister said Grace. Tea was at four and the bread was new and doughy, and had to be cut into hunks anyway, and supper was at half past eight, when one came off duty. It was usually sausages and disguised pies, and perhaps blancmange and cold rice pudding left over from dinner. One thing that hospital taught me was to eat all sorts of puddings I had been refusing since nursery. Hunger compelled it. My appetite grew enormous and I saw myself becoming one of the doorstop and dripping brigade, with my apron growing tighter each day and my dress straining at the seams.[4]

All probationer nurses put on weight during the first few months of their training due to the heavily loaded, carbohydrate-filled diet. Food and lodging were deducted from the probationer's pay packet at source and many hospitals cut food costs by feeding their nurses as cheaply as they could manage. Nursing was, and still is, a profession that required a lot of stamina and energy, and therefore it was considered appropriate to stave off the hunger pangs of young girls by filling them full of stodgy food. For some girls the combination of strict discipline, unfamiliar surroundings and poor-quality food increased their sense of homesickness, and the drop-out rate for young probationers was always highest during the first year of training.

Margot took to nursing like a duck to water. She had a practical common-sense approach to life and her physical stamina stood her in good stead. It was not long before she made some firm friends and developed a close camaraderie with fellow probationers Nancy Mitton and Jenny Kemsley. They supported each other wholeheartedly through the ups and downs of training school, and spent their off-duty hours and vacations gleefully sharing humorous stories, jokes and experiences. All three girls were mischievous, vibrant and adventurous.

The rigid conformity of hospital routines were like straitjackets on young would-be nurses and in off-duty periods, as nursing magazines advocated, they let their hair down as much as possible. Relaxation was always regulated to some extent by Matron, however, and certain pastimes were frowned upon. London probationers had an added bonus, in that the capital's theatres were in the habit of sending batches of complimentary tickets to nurses as a thank you gift for all their hard work. Margot, Nancy and Jenny took full advantage of these theatre gifts, and also managed to fit in the time to go riding, swimming and dancing. Margot was a big fan of Fats Waller and loved dancing to all forms of jazz music. The years she spent in nurse training may have been exhausting and demanding but they were also filled with fun, friendship and a sense of achievement.

In 1935 Margot successfully sat her final hospital exams and became a State Registered Nurse. She stayed at Bart's for a further six months to undergo theatre nurse training and was about to sign up for another six months when a chance meeting changed the course of her life. Nancy's sister Eleanor returned to Britain on leave from the Queen Alexandra's Royal Imperial Nursing Service (QAs), and during a weekend visit to Nancy's home Margot was introduced to Eleanor, who regaled her with stories of foreign travel and adventure. Margot listened avidly to these accounts of military nursing in different countries, cultures and lifestyles with a growing sense of fascination. She had always wanted to travel and explore the world and she quickly recognised that the QAs offered an ample opportunity for her to fulfil her ambition.

Rejecting a further contract with Bart's in favour of foreign adventure, Margot firmly set her sights on becoming an army nurse. She later claimed that she was also attracted by the QA uniform, which included bright red capes. Officially called tippets, the red capes were originally designed to hide the female sexuality from the ordinary 'Tommy' because army officers believed that a nurse's modesty needed protection from sexually deprived soldiers. With Margot's natural air of authority, however, it is unlikely that she needed such protection.

Margot began her six-month military probationary period at Cambridge Military Hospital, Aldershot, and was later gazetted and given a bronze medal to wear on her cape. This medal indicated her military staff nurse status. By Christmas 1937 she was working as a general nurse in Millbank Hospital and enjoying life in London once again. For a time she was allowed to ride the Life Guards' horses that were stabled at a riding school near Knightsbridge, and she also attended countless military ceremonies. But although Margot enjoyed being back in London she was impatient for an overseas posting. After all, she could hardly describe her QA journey, which thus far had taken her from London to Aldershot and back again, as being particularly adventurous. Since she was not allowed to request a posting, she simply had to wait her turn. Nearly a year later, in September 1938, the eagerly anticipated posting orders arrived. Margot was destined for Karachi, India, aboard a ship named *Neuralia*, a journey that would take three weeks to complete. This news delighted her immensely, and on 5 November she set sail with enthusiasm and joyful anticipation.

On the tortuous and lengthy route to Karachi, Margot was able to spend some time in Gibraltar, Malta and Aden while the ship refuelled and picked up more passengers. She finally disembarked with a sense of wonderment at her destination on 26 November. Entranced by the colours, smells and market place hum of Karachi, Margot was very reluctant to travel onwards to the small military station in Bareilly. This last leg of her journey encompassed the Sind Desert and Lahore. The train was uncomfortable and she was besieged by flies, intense heat and dust. Upon arrival, however, her initial impressions were favourable. Bareilly had a temperate climate in November, with beaming sunshine during the day and moderately chilly evenings. The area was covered with beautiful roses, sweet peas and zinnias, surrounded by lush green grass and foliage.

Added to this idyllic setting was a lavish colonial lifestyle which included purpose-built officers' clubs, large swimming pools, riding stables, tennis courts and cricket pitches. Military nurses in India worked extremely hard, sometimes in very difficult climatic conditions, but in peacetime they were able to revel in luxurious comfort. For Margot, India was everything she hoped it would be: colourful, exciting, interesting, spiritual and challenging. Professionally she was also very happy and acquired new technical skills by attending a specialist operating theatre course. Theatre nursing was an extremely stressful field of nursing and not all girls were up to the task. One young girl remembered that she approached her first days in the operating theatre with some trepidation:

I liked going to the theatre at night; it was exciting, and the operations, being nearly all emergency ones, were imbued with a sense of urgency. Also, there was only one theatre nurse on at night, so that the nurse who brought the patient from the ward had to assist in all the little things that the theatre staff did in the day time. When I ran about with the drums, brought in the saline bowl or held a leg I felt as important as if I were doing the whole operation. It was nerve-racking because I did not know what to do, and with a dangerously ill patient on the table, the atmosphere tense with the surgeon's nervous irritability and someone hissing from behind a mask, 'Quick Nurse! Give her an injection of atropine', I nearly had a stroke ... I personally was terrified of all surgeons and hated having to go near enough to do up their sterile gowns or to wipe the sweat from their brows. Once or twice I had touched them and made them un-sterile and I wished myself dead as I received their reaction at having to go through the whole scrubbing-up business again. My greatest shame, however, was when one of them suddenly shot at me through his mask: 'Fetch the proctoscope!' Never having heard of the instrument before, I heard it as something else and came trotting faithfully back with the white coat of the night porter which I had dragged off his indignant back.[5]

Fortunately, Margot did not experience such problems in the theatre environment. She had a cool, calm approach and an extensive knowledge of all theatre instruments and procedures, which she had gained from a studious application to her training. She was a professional, competent, reliable theatre sister who formed a crucial and valuable component of military operating theatre teams wherever she was posted. In India, she thrived in her nursing field, and the extra specialist courses that were laid on by the army stimulated her interest and maintained her professional development. In addition she had made a number of friends and had begun to feel at home. In these relaxing pre-war days Margot simply enjoyed all the facilities that the bustling British garrison had to offer.

Notes

1. Before the inauguration of the National Health Service, hospitals in Britain either operated within the voluntary sector or were run by local authorities. A two-tier system had evolved whereby voluntary hospitals were considered to be elite establishments, while those that were run by local authorities were viewed as being only a few steps away from the dreaded workhouses.
2. This marriage bar on women was eventually lifted during the Second World War because some professions, such as nursing and teaching, experienced extreme labour shortages. In certain occupations, however, in the higher echelons of the Civil Service for instance, the marriage bar remained until 1975.
3. M. Dickens, *One Pair of Feet* (1942), p. 10.
4. Ibid., pp. 24–5.
5. Ibid., pp. 85–6.

2

Nursing in India

There was no doubt that Margot loved every minute of her time in India, and the country was widely regarded by the British as 'the jewel in the crown' of the British Empire. During the interwar period public support for the empire was arguably at its strongest in British history. This support was bolstered by school education and empire days, popular literature, religious missionary societies, cinema film, newspaper and wireless stories, notions of imperial heroes and popular youth groups such as the scouting movement. National exhibitions were frequently held to propound the virtues and adventures of imperial conquests and to demonstrate the importance of empirical links.

British colonial acquisition began during the eighteenth century and by the turn of the twentieth century Britain possessed the largest overseas empire in history. This realm covered a quarter of the earth's habitable land, and a geographical area of over 12 million square miles was controlled by the British government. In terms of population, Britain and its empire contained around 400 million people, and 294 million of these lived in India. Clearly, economic and strategic interests had firmly bound Britain to its empire and vice versa, but there were signs that the ties were loosening by the 1930s.

The First World War had given impetus to Indian nationalist movements and eventually, in response to nationalist pressure from the Indian National Congress and Indian religious leader Gandhi, Britain implemented a series of cautious administrative reforms in India. But for a growing number of Indians these were not enough, and nationalist movements became more violent and vocal. An Indian named Subhas Chandra Bose, who was educated in Britain at Cambridge University, became a leading protagonist within these movements and established an Indian National Army. Despite interwar popularity and media reinforcement of the empire, the roots of decolonisation were already visible.

The economic rationale for supporting the empire was being called into question, and from the First World War onwards Indian nationalist campaigns boycotted imported cloth and made it difficult for cloth manufacturers in Lancashire to recover their lost markets. Attempts were made to rejuvenate British trade with India but the long interwar depression had hampered these and investors began to look elsewhere for more lucrative markets. Members of the Indian Civil Service and the Colonial Service still relied on the empire for their livelihoods and good relationships with the Raj were maintained. But India was also on the road to self-sufficiency and self-government. British politicians had not yet constructed a timetable for giving India independence, but there was a growing recognition that eventually Britain would have to relinquish its jewel in the empire's crown. Up until 1945, however, Britain still maintained a heavy military presence within its colonial territories.

British military hospitals in India fell into two categories: those that were primarily designated for colonial Indian troops and their families; and those that catered for British officers, soldiers and their family members. Aside from the usual medical and surgical emergencies, the main medical conditions in India were smallpox, typhoid, cholera and malaria. Matrons were always keen to instruct nurses on the safety protocols for working in such extreme heat, and lectured new arrivals on the importance of drinking enough clear fluids, appropriate drinking water and the crucial habit of wearing a hat at all times when outdoors. Sunstroke was a very real and dangerous affliction for the unwary and careless.

The small hospital in Bareilly where Margot was stationed catered for British military personnel and was staffed by one matron, six QAs and two or three medical officers. Indian sepoys did much of the general cleaning work and the strict Indian caste system meant there were often problems with regard to task allocation. Sometimes nurses were sent into remote areas to care for individual patients with infectious or communicable diseases and this policy brought its own set of problems. This isolationist approach made considerable sense in that it contained the spread of disease, but often its implementation depended on staffing levels. Remote areas also presented obstacles in terms of travel. For instance, when Margot was sent to a hill station for a month to care for a civilian surgeon, she had to be carried up the bumpy, shrub-ridden hillside by sedan chair because the hill tracks were too narrow and inaccessible.

The British military had constructed several tiny hill stations to compensate for the fact that many people could not make the journey to hospital. These hill stations were dotted about the United Provinces. But in some instances, even when patients could make the journey to a main hospital, it was not appropriate for them to do so. Patients with highly infectious diseases needed to be nursed in total isolation to prevent epidemics and on one occasion Margot was sent nearly 200 miles away to Meerut to care for a lady who was suffering from smallpox.

All military personnel and their families were offered vaccinations against this potentially fatal disease, but this particular lady, an officer's wife, had refused the vaccination. Against the odds, and largely due to the excellent nursing care that Margot provided, the lady did survive, although it was impossible for the sensible, level-headed Margot to understand why anyone would knowingly put their lives at risk by refusing to be vaccinated against proven fatal diseases. Nevertheless, it was not her place to cast judgement. Margot was patient, even-tempered and took most things in her stride. While she undoubtedly harboured reservations about the wisdom of some people's actions, she always dealt with the medical consequences in a cool, professional manner. Above all, she continually attempted to make the best of a bad or difficult situation. Nurses generally, and military nurses in particular, were adept at hiding, suppressing and controlling their emotions. They were required to cultivate an effective emotional barrier in order to adequately care for their patients, and Margot was no exception. Indeed, following the death of her father she had realised, perhaps more than most, the value of self-control and self-discipline. She considered displays of emotion to be a sign of weakness and self-indulgence. The nurses' uniforms also played a part in this emotional control process by acting as a visible and physical barrier, and providing wearers with some distance from individual, sensitive scenarios.

Obviously these emotional barriers did not mean for one minute that Margot was immune to the normal range of feelings that everyone else experienced; they merely provided her with an effective method of suppressing and dealing with them, which allowed her to continue with her work unhindered. Emotions were then acknowledged and confronted in a private manner away from prying or potentially interfering eyes. Whenever Margot succumbed to melancholic thoughts, she tended to reprimand herself relatively quickly and simply got on with life. She always felt that she had a firm sense of direction and her everyday work association with the sick and wounded made her appreciate life more fully.

She loved travel. India, with its fascinating landscape, history, culture and people, never ceased to amaze the ever-inquisitive Margot, and she took the opportunity in particular to discover the history of Meerut and its people. As part of this process she walked purposefully around the numerous Indian cemeteries at dusk, carefully reading the gravestone inscriptions. Hundreds of men, women and children were buried in these meticulously kept cemeteries, because Meerut was the site of the famous Indian Mutiny of 1857.

Between July and October 1939 Margot moved to Ranikhet Hospital which she loved with a passion. From the hospital rooftop it was possible to view a spectacular sunrise over the Himalayas. Mount Everest was just out of sight but there were breathtaking and magnificent views of the majestic peaks of Nanda, Devi and Nanga Parbat. Margot never tired of this breathtaking scenery and religiously climbed each morning to the rooftop to eagerly await the dawn. There was a golf course behind the hospital and in her off-duty hours she took full advantage of this facility. She also rode some ponies that were owned by Maharajah Reiwar. He was attached to the British garrison and his son spent his days training the ponies for the game of polo. The nurses happily offered to exercise them on a daily basis. But this arrangement only lasted for two months because the maharajah's son contracted cerebral malaria and tragically died. The distraught maharajah was inconsolable and could no longer care for the polo ponies because they were a constant reminder of his son.

Cerebral malaria was rare compared to other forms of the disease and there was no medication to halt its progress; affected patients usually died within hours of diagnosis. Medical experiments were conducted in India in 1932 on monkeys with malaria and these demonstrated that the monkey malaria strain named *plasmodium knowlesi* produced no symptoms in Indian rhesus monkeys but was fatal to the Malayan monkeys. This form of malaria produced a twenty-four-hour fever in humans from which they usually recovered. There were numerous varieties of malaria, however, and very little in the way of protection. Colonials had long been advised to drink gin and tonic because the quinine in the tonic water offered some protection against the disease. A German pharmaceutical company had produced some synthetic anti-malarial drugs but these were not available to British medical personnel at this stage.[1]

In September 1939 Margot, along with others in her hill station, gathered round the well-travelled, battered old hospital wireless and listened to Neville Chamberlain's speech that announced the outbreak of war between Britain and Germany. By this stage she was quite settled and contented in India, having bought herself a 10-year-old Austin 7 car and a dachshund puppy. She was also receiving a comfortable salary of £80 a year basic pay that was topped up by her Indian overseas increment of £20 a year. Until this point, her life in India had been dominated by hard work combined with an immense sense of pleasure. But now she was able to travel around the countryside admiring the stunning views, getting to know the Indian people, and learning more about their philosophy and religious beliefs. Often she travelled long distances by pony and cart, a form of transport that was known as a tum tum. This was an enthralling time for all of the young QAs, many of whom had never travelled outside Britain before their postings to the far-flung 'jewel in the empire's crown'. Furthermore, the colonial clubs and sports facilities shielded the officers, nurses and their patients from the cruelties of the outside world. One of Margot's nursing colleagues described the situation aptly:

Northern India was a place so attractive and peaceful that it was difficult to credit that a Second World War was beginning, even with the wireless announcements reminding us of the fact from time to time. For two years I divided my time between the plain and hill stations, longing, like everybody else, to be sent on active service, listening to the wireless accounts of the tragedies of that period, and feeling that our families at home were getting more of the knocks of war than we were. At the same time we realised that the work we were doing in India, though on the surface less spectacular, was growing daily in importance. Practically all the British personnel were removed from our hospitals and their place taken by Anglo-Indians, all of whom had to be trained as quickly and efficiently as possible into useful members of the Royal Army Medical Corps. Members of the Auxiliary Nursing Service, India, also came to help us and to receive instructions. At times we gave lectures to Indian orderlies from the local Indian Military Hospital where no sisters were employed and, personally, I found them all intensely keen, many very intelligent.[2]

The winter of 1939 was a strange one for many of the military nurses. In one sense they all felt as though they were in limbo, waiting for more important instructions that would take them closer to the battlefields of war and nearer to the soldiers that needed their care. This particular winter was also a very severe one:

We were very full all that winter, an exceptionally severe one. Large convoys came down from the North, scores of Indians falling victims to frost bite, owing to the unusual conditions, many losing their toes, a few their limbs.[3]

Military medical staff based in India were initially protected from the harsh realities of the Second World War, but in Britain the medical and nursing services were plunged into chaos. The situation was compounded by inept government policy and the subordination of civilian healthcare needs to those of the emergency services. Staff at voluntary hospitals were conscripted and subjected to the jurisdiction of the Ministry of Health, and the outpatient departments of such hospitals disappeared virtually overnight. Margot's beloved Bart's, where she had completed her nurse training, had only 145 beds available for civilian patients out of a total of 780.

While the situation was less severe in rural locations, the ratio of bed allocation for civilians posed problems in several major areas. Official figures estimated that 10 million people attended voluntary hospitals every year and the absence of outpatient clinics placed a substantial burden on district nursing services. Dire notices were erected across the nurses' homes as an atmosphere of paranoia gripped the country. Most of these were concerned with blackout regulations and solemnly pointed out that not adhering to these regulations was treacherous and unpatriotic; others were more effusive. Some exclaimed that nurses should not talk to anyone on public transport, not go out walking in parks and not attend social meetings of any kind. A matron at the Royal London Hospital was even accused of trying to communicate with the enemy by hanging out her bed sheets on the hospital roof in a certain order on different days.

The government introduced an emergency hospital scheme and a casualty clearing system, but the need to recruit, train and deploy nurses in adequate numbers for the duration of the war presented the government with a problem which was never fully resolved. From the outbreak of war onwards women were required to work in a myriad of different industries, as one young woman recorded with some humour:

One had got to be something; that was obvious. But what? It seemed that women, having been surplus for twenty years, were suddenly wanted in a hundred different places at once. You couldn't open a newspaper without being told that YOU were wanted in the Army, the Navy or the Air Force; factory wheels would stop turning unless you rushed into overalls at once; the AFS could quench no fires without you, every hording beckoned you and even Marble Arch badgered you about the ARP. The Suffragettes could have saved themselves a lot of trouble if they had seen this coming. Men's jobs were open to women and trousers were selling like hot cakes on Kensington High Street.[4]

Opportunities for women were suddenly unleashed but they did not always have an easy time proving their worth. A number of them complained about sexism and patronising attitudes, yet for some, preconceived ideas about female capabilities merely served to act as a challenge. One woman recalled how changing the attitude of a hostile lieutenant eventually made her ill:

> He didn't like the Wrens ... women doing a man's job ... He thought he'd give us a challenge, and he said, 'you see that frame over there?' 'Yes Sir.' 'That's a Swordfish frame. Build it!' So I went back to my crew, to the girls, and I said, 'five of us have got to build that Swordfish'. Which is a joke, but we set to. We had one leading hand to help us, and we set to. It took us weeks, months, but we got it, from scratch. From just the fuselage frame ... I took over the job of splicing steel cable for the flying wires and control wires. And oh, my fingers were sore, they bled, but we were going to show this lieutenant what we could do. It took us months, but we did it, and it flew. Put me in [the] sick-bay for a fortnight, I had a nervous breakdown. But it was very satisfying. It was very, very satisfying to know that it flew.[5]

Despite the prevalence of patronising attitudes in some industrial work fields, some women recalled how they were actually treated with respect and kindness:

> Really we were cared for, we were pampered, we were looked after, all the men were so kind to us, you know, there was no nastiness at all, they were so kind to us; they were protective towards us and all this. And at the ATS Headquarters at Bedbury ... they thought, 'those poor girls out in the wild', you know, 'life is hard for them', whereas we were having a whale of a time because although we worked quite hard, as I say, we had such lovely friendships with people there and they were so kind to us, and it was really very nice.[6]

In terms of how women were received into the workforce, therefore, individual situations were a lottery. There were stories of oppression but equally stories of support, encouragement and admiration for their efforts to step into the brink and undertake men's work. Moreover, it was not surprising that this vast and new array of wartime work opportunities for women had severely curtailed efforts to recruit young girls into the nursing profession. By comparison, industrial work paid women higher salaries for less working hours. Nursing services were diluted with untrained personnel immediately when war was declared and recruitment was viewed in terms of overall figures with no regard for proficiency levels. For those girls who had embarked on a course to gain nurse registration there was very little in the way of financial recompense for their lengthy period of training:

> The war, of course, sends a lot of girls into hospital, but in normal times, apart from hero-worship and a semi-religious call, they go because nursing is about the only profession which you can enter entirely unqualified and not only get your training free but be paid while you are training. I never can see that nurses are so underpaid in the probationer stage. Besides their training, they get their keep, uniform and all their medical treatment for nothing. I agree that the wages of a fully trained nurse are iniquitous; their skill and experience, acquired after three years of comparative slavery, should entitle them to more pay than a high-class parlour maid. I say all this now, rather smugly, but at the time, of course, I grumbled as much as anyone and disparaged the contents of my monthly envelope.[7]

The problem was not helped by a Ministry of Health policy that assumed all women could nurse because nursing was simply an extension of mothering. Members of the civilian nursing profession responded to this slight by focusing on ways to elevate their status, and military nurses strove to resolve the ambiguity of their position within the armed forces. In an attempt to protect their status, no regulars were recruited into the military nursing services during the war. Therefore, they were heavily outnumbered by reserve nurses. The Queen Alexandra's Imperial Military Nursing Service (QAIMNS) expanded from 624 to 12,000; the Queen Alexandra's Royal Naval Nursing Service (QARNNS) from 78 to 1,341; and the Princess Mary's Royal Air Force Nursing Service (PMRAFNS) from 171 to a total of 1,215 members.

British military nursing services had a long and honourable history that stemmed from Florence Nightingale and the Crimean War, and were considered to be the nursing elite. They were the only female units to be retained by the armed forces at the end of the First World War. However, despite their undoubted prestige, their position within the armed forces was always ambiguous. From 1939 onwards, the arrival of the women's Auxiliary Territorial Service (ATS) threatened to undermine the long-standing status of military nursing services. In terms of pay and working conditions, the ATS fared better than military nurses by assimilating to the army rank pattern from the outset. This fact was not lost on the matron-in-chief, Dame Katherine Jones, who followed suit and advocated the immediate and total assimilation of her nurses to the army rank pattern. Along with this militarisation policy, Jones also pushed her nurses further and further towards the front line in an attempt to get commissioned officer status for all military registered nurses. This goal was achieved in 1941.

In the meantime, Margot was dealing with status problems of an entirely different nature, and these were inextricably bound up with the Indian caste system:

The natives are divided into caste and class, and I believe it is the most difficult thing for anyone born, say, in the sweeper family to get into the bearer family. You meet it everywhere – in the wards we have orderlies (some English, some Anglo-Indian), who 'do' for the patient; we have ward boys, who are the senior of the servants, and have everything to do with food and dusting the wards, ordering the goods, etc. We have Beasties, who fetch and carry water and do the screening, and Sweepers, who sweep and white wash your walls, and clean the patients' boots, etc. Try and get the ward boy to fetch in a bowl of water, or an orderly to fetch a patient a dinner: he will feed the patient with it but not fetch it. Ask the Beastie to pick up some fluff – he shouts for the ward boy, and he for the Sweeper, and they all shout together.[8]

India's strict caste system affected task allocation on a daily basis. Sweepers were happy to sweep, deal with latrines, bedpans, soiled linen and water, while the beasties would only deal with clean linen and water. Ward boys would only deal with food and feeding utensils, and sepoys could be relied upon to make beds but little else. They had an intense dislike of touching dead bodies and refused point-blank to help with any direct patient care. These practical problems were often compounded by language difficulties and many ward sisters introduced simple sign language techniques for issuing instructions.

Night duty also raised some eyebrows and prompted protests from Indian nationals. As far as the latter were concerned it was simply not the done thing to have women working at night. Cultural tradition forbade women to be out after dark, and British military nurses found themselves bombarded with frantic and sometimes hysterical objections from Indian medical staff, who claimed female night nurses were in extreme danger of losing both their virtue and reputation. This problem was only resolved by constant reassurances from the British High Command and by individual night sisters dogmatically insisting on their absolute need to run the wards and be responsible for their patients at night. However, as the days sped by in a whirl of hospital activity, it was remarkable how quickly cultural and language difficulties dissipated as the British military sisters and Indian staff developed their communication skills.

Margot picked up some of the Indian language and acquired a good deal of knowledge about tropical diseases and Indian culture, but with the outbreak of war she had grown increasingly restless. At the time of the Dunkirk retreat she requested permission to go on active service. This request was politely refused. There was an extreme shortage of qualified theatre sisters in India and since Margot was one of the few who had studied the specialist army theatre courses, she was too valuable to send on active service until more sisters had undertaken the training. To ease her restlessness her superiors suggested that she take a holiday instead, and they assured her that she would be better equipped to deal with eventual active service if she was well rested before the event. Reluctantly, Margot agreed and embarked on a travelling holiday with her friend Dorothy, who was stationed at Lucklow. They both had an adventurous and relaxing time, visiting the Bay of Bengal, Calcutta, Delhi and Agra.

Margot kept abreast of the international news as best she could and her long-awaited orders to go on active service eventually arrived in

February 1941, asking her to report to Bombay on 1 March for a posting with No 17 Combined General Hospital. She quickly sold her car, placed her belongings in storage and found a suitable home for her beloved dachshund.

Together with eight other QA sisters, Margot arrived in Bombay at the appointed time. The ship was not ready to embark so they were all housed for a very tense week in the Grand Hotel. Margot befriended and shared a room with another QA called Eileen Gibbs, who she quickly nicknamed Kiwi because of her New Zealand roots. They left Bombay harbour on 8 March accompanied by an assortment of other military personnel. These included the Indian Infantry Battalion, Mysore Infantry of the Indian State Forces and No 17 Combined General Hospital. The largest numbers of hospital personnel were Indian and included sixteen Indian nursing sisters, eight QAs of the British section, four Royal Army Medical Corps (RAMC) officers and one matron. The commanding officer was a British man of the Indian Medical Service (IMS) and most of the others were British and Indian officers of the IMS.

The ship had been travelling for over twelve hours before the ship's captain opened his top-secret orders at midnight on 8/9 March, and announced to his passengers and crew that they were bound for the fortress island of Singapore. The British colonial island was a flourishing international port that lay at the strategic crossroads of the Indian and Pacific Oceans and the South China Sea. Thus it linked the industrial Western world with the developing resources of colonial Asia. A railway transport system ensured that Malayan tin, rubber and iron ore reached the docks via the Straits of Johore and was unloaded in the southern region of the island. The city was well organised and the centre and harbour area reflected its colonial status, with large government buildings and landscaped ornate parks.

Upon arrival the QAs were transported by train to Kuala Lumpur, which was about a third of the way up the Malayan peninsula. From here they travelled to Tanjong Malim, where they took up residence in a large Malayan teaching hospital that was surrounded by bungalows. They had a long wait before their work could begin, since it took three weeks for the equipment, troops, medical supplies and patients to catch up with them. Margot wrote home to her beloved mother with her usual wry sense of humour, stating that for someone on active service she had never been quite as inactive in all her life![9]

Notes

1. The synthetic anti-malarial drug Sontochin was only acquired by the Allies when Tunis was liberated by the Americans in 1943.
2. The National Archives War Office Files, WO 222/189/10.
3. Ibid.
4. M. Dickens, *One Pair of Feet* (1942), p. 1.
5. P. Summerfield, *Reconstructing Women's Wartime Lives* (1998), p. 133.
6. Ibid., p. 144.
7. Dickens, *One Pair of Feet*, p. 38.
8. Royal London Hospital Nurses' League Review, Nos ix and x (1940–41).
9. Imperial War Museum Oral History Interview with Dame Margot Turner, ref. 9126.

3

Japanese Expansion

Following the fall of France in the spring of 1940 the northern part of French Indo-China was occupied by the Japanese, who had taken the opportunity to expand their empire. By the time Margot arrived in Singapore in March 1941, therefore, the Japanese were already based near Malaya. For tactical purposes the Japanese had also signed a tripartite agreement with Germany and Italy. But in the early days of Margot's stint in Singapore, British colonial life continued much as it always had done, seemingly unaware of the Japanese threat on the doorstep. There was a total conviction amongst British officers and their men that nothing untoward could ever damage the superb and lavish lifestyle of colonials in South-East Asia.

Singapore was viewed by the British as an impregnable fortress both at home and abroad. British officers had achieved good relationships with the native population and administered the colony with tact and efficiency. Nevertheless, Singapore had a mixed reputation in terms of business activities, and a less than salubrious one in many quarters. Prostitution had been a considerable problem on the island since the nineteenth century and this pleasure dome of vice had prompted an epidemic of venereal disease amongst British troops. Even Government House played host to a variety of unofficial and illegal parties, and young native girls were expected to entertain visiting dignitaries.

Yet alongside the precarious, undercover world of vice, gambling, corruption, exploitation and various forms of racketeering by dubious characters, lay another, more genteel society; one that was permeated with slightly arrogant notions of colonial and racial superiority, and exuded superficial politeness and good breeding. A society that was extravagant and occasionally exploitative but less obviously corrupt.

For the young nurse Margot, Singapore was a melting pot of confusing contrasts, a tumultuous world of exciting and unfamiliar sights, sounds and tastes. She also found that senior British officers were extremely knowledgeable about the history and culture of the island and were happy to act as her guides. Off-duty hours were spent in a whirlwind of social activity: horse riding, lawn tennis tournaments, cricket matches and a never-ending series of elite communal gatherings at the ostentatious and world famous Raffles hotel.

Raffles was founded in 1819 and lay at the very centre of high-class colonial living. Lavish parties, ceremonial celebrations, anniversary dances and gourmet dinners were all part and parcel of everyday life for the colonial officers and their clan. Ladies gossiped in the luxurious Raffles powder room, sipped gin and tonic on the hotel terrace, and discussed their make-up and fashion accessories as though nothing else in the world mattered. This female world of high society was light years away from that of the practical and forthright Margot, who viewed the preening and pontificating of such women with a degree of concealed amusement. She was also quite astonished to discover that people thought nothing of travelling to Raffles from Kuala Lumpur simply for a good night out, and had remarked as much to Colonel Hurford when he gave her a lift back to the hospital after a particularly rousing jazz concert one evening.

But whenever the subject of war cropped up in conversation, calm, measured reassurances were the order of the day. British propaganda portrayed Singapore, and indeed the whole of Malaya, as being invincible to enemy attack. Despite considerable and mounting evidence to the contrary, British colonial life in South-East Asia, slightly deluded and partially shielded from reality, continued as normal.

In these relatively peaceful wartime days Margot and her friend Kiwi even managed to go on holiday to an Australian Red Cross base at Frazer's Hill. Here they enjoyed long, relaxing woodland walks and played several rounds of golf. The work at the hospital was steady but not hectic, and occasionally patients were brought down from the 20th General Combined Hospital in Taiping to use the hospital's x-ray equipment. This process gave the nursing sisters time to exchange news about each other's hospitals and discuss medical supplies and patient progress. It also gave them a chance to discuss progress and changes in nursing practice.

The Second World War differed dramatically from earlier conflicts in that it covered a much wider geographical area and was highly mobile in nature. Each battle scenario was dictated by new weapon technology and the peculiar circumstances of each new theatre of war. For instance, whereas in previous wars field ambulances had always followed the brigades, in this conflict they were situated at the front line. More vehicles were lost by adopting this strategy but more lives were saved. The need to maintain troop movement was paramount. Medical units were smaller and more flexible, and dressing stations were located as near to the front line as possible in order to attend to more wounded but not impede the fighting forces. Rapid developments in blood transfusion and plastic surgery ensured that many more lives were saved and standards of care for the armed forces continually improved.

The nature of wounds had also changed, since this war was increasingly fought from the air. The rapid speed with which aeroplanes on fire hurtled to the ground produced what became known as 'airman's burns'. These burns caused deep penetration and the destruction of body tissues, and were initially treated by sulphonamide powder and Vaseline gauze. Eventually less painful methods of treating burns were introduced, such as the irrigation bag. Affected limbs were simply floated in a bag that was filled with salt water (saline); this process provided a continuous antiseptic and painless treatment that allowed the limbs to heal.

In addition to their physical injuries, pilots and air crew were also prone to psychological stress. This problem was not always immediately obvious but became a recognised potential consequence of battle. When pilots crashed their aircraft the crew were either killed instantly, suffered severe burns, or were found sitting calmly by the wreckage of their aeroplanes having a cigarette. Research into the stress levels of air crew discovered that it was the gunner rather than the pilot who suffered higher anxiety levels, because he was a 'sitting duck' in many respects. In stark contrast to attitudes in previous conflicts, research demonstrated that sufferers of battle stress could be rehabilitated by positive psychotherapy. Later medical developments in pharmacology, such as penicillin, also helped with the treatment and recovery of injured military personnel.

Traditionally, in the area where Margot was nursing in the tropics, loss of life from sickness and disease always exceeded the number of troops who died as a direct result of battle. Preventative medicine was crucial in this theatre of war. The consultant physician to South-East Asia Command estimated that four-fifths of the sickness in this area could be prevented by good anti-malaria discipline, and stated: 'One officer engaged on hygiene can save the work of ten medical officers in hospital.'[1]

New methods of immunisation, anti-malaria drugs and insecticide development all eventually combined to assist the British and Allied armed forces in their fight against malaria. Scrub typhus was also a problem and a vaccine was developed. Its efficiency, however, was not proven and the Medical Research Council issued the following advice:

1. The avoidance of recent jungle and cultivated land.
2. Camps to be provided with paths and tents with floors.
3. Placing seats, beds and hammocks more than one foot from the ground (i.e. the limit of the mite's climbing ability). The avoidance of lying on the ground. A groundsheet cannot be relied upon to give protection from the ground.
4. Bulldozing the surface of camp sites, and burning of scrub or grass were of little value and DDT did not appear to be insecticidal to Trombicula.[2]

Undoubtedly the fight against disease was in many respects as important as the fight against the enemy. For Margot, these balmy days of professional discussions with colleagues about changes in medical and nursing practice represented the calm before the storm. Aside from those who were suffering from some form of tropical disease, the patients suffered from routine, everyday conditions, such as chest infections, in-growing toenails, abscesses, appendicitis and other abdominal conditions. But everything changed when the Japanese attacked Pearl Harbor on 7 December 1941. Following the threat of an American oil embargo and running short of its own supplies, Japanese ministers and senior military personnel had convened on 4 September to draw up plans to attack the American Pacific fleet. Their primary objective was to render the United States fleet inactive; once this was achieved they could go ahead and establish a long sought-after expansion of their empire in South-East Asia. Japanese ministers also intended to form a series of defensible territories in the area to act as buffer zones. The subsequent surprise Pearl Harbor attack effectively destroyed the American Pacific fleet and Japan declared war on America and Britain.

The following day Japanese forces landed in Thailand and Malaya, and the first bombs landed on Singapore. From this point on the Japanese swept through European colonial outposts at an alarming rate. Their forces had achieved cohesion of purpose and their Bushido code made them a formidable enemy. The code effectively stated that it was wrong to surrender to the enemy under any circumstances, and it was better for a Japanese soldier to end his life in battle or commit suicide rather than be taken prisoner. For Japanese soldiers this code of honour was always uppermost in their minds as they ventured into battle. They had no regard for the enemy and a total lack of respect for their womenfolk.

Mrs Fidoe, a nurse working at St Stephen's College in Hong Kong at the time of the Japanese invasion, graphically described the event:

There was sniping and shelling going on all day long. The patients were all in the main hall and the staff were – the majority of them – gathered outside. There was shelling all night. About quarter to seven – it was difficult to know the time, it was dark in the morning – we suddenly heard shots and cries. I thought at first that one of our own men had gone mad as there were one or two of them who had shell shock. I then realised that bayonets were poking through the blanket curtains covering the doors. The Japanese had come into the small hall and staircase and up the other side. They ran up the staircase and got amongst us and seemed to be more concerned in taking all our jewellery. The first thing I knew was that a man had his arms up my sleeve and had taken all my jewellery. Then they burst down into the main hall.

There was a small room leading off the hall and they bundled us into that small room and locked us up. There were quite a number of dead bodies lying in pools of blood. I think there were about thirty of us in that room, patients and nurses. After we had been there for about two hours, the Japanese opened the door and ordered us all out and to go upstairs. This wounded soldier had crawled out of the main hall with his splint hanging off and had dragged himself into that room. He was also ordered upstairs with us. He could not walk and I had to put my arm on his elbow and help him. A Japanese shouted at me and beat me up. He beat my arm with the butt end of a rifle. On the first floor we were all divided up and forced into little rooms. All day long Japanese soldiers came in and out of the room. They stood staring at us and searched us for any valuables we might have and we heard screams coming from various parts of the building. It would be difficult to describe where the screaming was coming from. There was a young Canadian soldier in the room with me. He had a wound in his arm and had been bayoneted again. We asked for bandages but they refused to give them to us.

At about that time (Christmas Day, 1941) two Japanese soldiers came along and made us, the nurses, stand up. They looked us up and down for half an hour and took away one and she did not come back. After a while they came back and beckoned to the two of us left and made us follow them along the corridor into a small room which I learned was one of the master's studies and left us there. The small study we were shown into had some Chinese women there when we got there. I think there were five.

These Chinese women, two of them were crying and there was a small bathroom out of the room and Japanese soldiers came and took them one after the other into the bathroom. They tried to resist but could not. This lasted about an hour. There were two mattresses on the floor. We thought we were going to be left there for the night to rest. A little afterwards a Japanese soldier came into the room and asked for one of us to go and bandage the wounded soldiers. One of us would not go without the other and Miss Gordan, Nursing Sister, myself and two VADs (Voluntary Aid Detatchment nurses), insisted on going together. We followed these soldiers along the corridor and they took us to a small room with mattresses on the floor and proceeded to rape us too.

I would say that while the soldiers were in there with us, another was standing with fixed bayonet outside the door, and suddenly the door was thrown open and the soldier beckoned to the others and they hurried us away along the corridor. They took us back to the room we had left formerly. There were no Chinese women there any more. They had all gone. There were just four of us there and we shut the door. The mattresses had also been taken away. It was quite empty. We stayed in that room all night, being visited by Japanese soldiers until we were so distraught that we would not open the door any more. We were raped from time to time. Every time a soldier left – the door had a slip lock – we locked it. We were so upset we just did not care what happened and would not open the door. They thought there was some of their own in there so they left us alone for two hours. There was a window looking out of the room where we stood and we watched the Japanese taking out mattresses, blankets and bodies and putting them on lorries and covering them up with blankets. I could not see who they were.

I saw them taking tables and chairs from the college and building up a huge mound which they set fire to. I saw them putting the dead bodies on the fire. Sometime after daybreak we heard footsteps and then the dental surgeon, Colonel McCurdie, knocked at the door together with a Japanese officer and some Japanese soldiers. Colonel McCurdie told us two of our own wounded were downstairs and he wanted us to go down and attend to them. He was only a dental surgeon. He was not a doctor. We went down and found two Canadian soldiers with small injuries in their feet and wrists. They had walked to the hospital over the hills, not knowing that we had surrendered.

We rendered first aid to the two Canadian soldiers and then we were told to go back upstairs and we could attend to our wounded. When we got back up there we found that all the rooms had been opened up and everyone was in the process of cleaning the place. There were lots of feathers about. We went down on our hands and knees and cleaned the place until dark. We found among the feathers some dead bodies. We then got some first-aid equipment from the store room downstairs and we attended the wounded.

We found in every case the splints had been taken off, the bandages had been cut and many of the men were bleeding rather badly and quite a few had bayonet wounds all over them.

This volunteer officer took us away about 5 o'clock. We had, with some medical orderlies, dressed most of their wounds before we left. We then went up to the fort. I have overlooked one thing. When we were called upstairs to attend the wounded, the husband of one of the volunteer nurses came and asked me if I knew where his wife was. She had been the one taken out of my room. The name was Begg. He asked if I knew where she was. I told him that she had been taken away. He came back with a Japanese officer and went round to search for her. He then came back and asked me to go with the Japanese officer. We met the Canadian padre and together with an orderly went down to the gardens and the other side of the nullah. The Japanese would not let anybody cross except me. There was a blanket by the bushes. I lifted the blanket and saw the bodies of three volunteer nurses. One was the body of Mrs Begg, the wife of the husband I spoke about, another Mrs Smith and the other Mrs Buxton. They were stripped, devoid of all clothing, except for a coat belonging to Mrs Buxton which was thrown over the bodies. Mrs Begg had been shot. There was a definite wound in her head. I saw throat wounds on the other two. It looked as though they had clean cuts through them. I saw the Japanese collect these bodies and put them on the funeral pyre. I went back to where Captain Barnett and the RAMC orderly were waiting. I went to pieces a little bit. The Japanese officer – he was very young – shook me. He said 'you lucky. Three minutes and you would have gone too. Hong Kong surrendered just in time.' Those were his words.[3]

Mrs Fidoe's experience was not an isolated one. Mrs Amy Williams was matron at the Jockey Relief Hospital on 25 December 1941 and recounted a similar story:

Three Japanese came along with bayonets and one had a hand grenade and one had a revolver as well as a bayonet. They told us to stand up. There were some lying on the floor. They went round us with a torch. He chose five girls and told them to go along with him. During the afternoon, all the Chinese bar two nurses and one doctor had disappeared. We had increased in staff by this time. When the air raid shelters were bombed out, they sent staff to us to house them. We had by this time 195 staff, chiefly, of course, Chinese. During the afternoon when they realised what was happening, they disappeared. By evening time we only had two nurses and one doctor and they escaped in the night. Of the five they released two of those girls. They raped three only of that lot. Afterwards they came down again and took four more up. In all, six Europeans were raped, two of them twice. After these happenings it was quiet until the next day. Then about 12 o'clock one of the Japanese came in and took one of the girls, dragging her by the arm through the ward. An officer appeared at the far end of the ward and he dropped her quickly and she fell on the bed. That was the end of the rape.[4]

It was clear that the attacks on the nurses were premeditated. One Japanese soldier named Ochi recalled a conversation with his comrade Yasu that went something as follows:

'That white thing up there is a hospital. Perhaps if you find some pretty little nurses, please think of me and spare me one. But no native nurse, please. Spare me a white one, a tight one, one that fits your taste.'
Then he looked back up at the hospital. Suddenly shots were fired up there. Shots from all directions, it seemed, fierce rapid fire. After three minutes it was all over. What had happened? Surely Yasu was in luck. He must have found some Eurasian nurses and was returning with one over his shoulder. He would soon be thrusting into the city together with his friend.[5]

News of these atrocities reverberated through the British colonies. They were all the more poignant because they were committed on Christmas Day and against unarmed medical personnel, many of whom were wearing the Red Cross symbol of neutrality at the time. The callous treatment of British women and nurses in particular astounded British military personnel. Policy directives were hurriedly issued to protect all military nurses from further harm, and instructions were sent to Singapore to facilitate the evacuation of nurses as a priority should Japanese forces land on the island.

Lengthy reports outlined the atrocities in gruesome detail. Certainly there was a barbaric Japanese mindset towards women of enemy races at this time, but cultural traditions suggested that Japanese men were not overly kind to women of their own race. According to Japanese doctrine, women were viewed as inferior to men because they all had five fundamental character flaws. Published as a revered guide for all Japanese men and used as a justification for their supposed superiority, the *Onna Daigaku: The Whole Duty of Woman* outlined the premise: 'The five faults that beset the female mind are: indocility, discontent, slander, jealousy and silliness. Without doubt these faults exist in seven or eight out of every ten women, and it is from these stems the inferiority of women to men.'[6]

Japanese military men did not for one second contemplate the possibility that these same five faults were manifestly apparent in some of their male military policies. All character failings were firmly laid at the door of their womenfolk.

As Japanese forces swept across the Pacific there was a mixed reaction in British political circles. Members of the British wartime coalition government did not appear to be unduly surprised by the surrender of Hong Kong. However, many politicians continued to believe that Singapore was an impregnable fortress. British Prime Minister Winston Churchill admitted privately that he did not think the island could withstand a Japanese assault for any length of time. Churchill had replaced Neville Chamberlain after the Dunkirk retreat and he was adamant that the war against Hitler's Nazis should take precedence over any Far Eastern endeavour. Furthermore, he was convinced that Burma was of more strategic importance than Singapore in terms of the overall war effort.

Burma was situated on the land road to India and was a vital reinforcement link to China. Both the American President Roosevelt and Churchill were concerned that if Burma was lost, the Chinese might relinquish the fight against Japan and consider joining forces with them instead. This development would contain the seeds of a major pan-Asiatic force. This fear was shared by the Australians, who were extremely alarmed by the advancing Japanese forces and the lack of British reinforcements. Despite protestations to the contrary, it was clear that Churchill had put the Pacific War on a backburner until the war in Europe had been settled. He did not underestimate the Japanese threat, he simply chose to defend Britain first and foremost, and place colonial interests second. But given this firm strategic policy, the fate of Singapore was effectively sealed long before the futile defence of the island began.

Notes

1. Lessons of the Second World War Official Royal Naval Medical Service website: www.royal-marines.mod.uk. The rate of preventable diseases in the early phases of the Japanese war exceeded 100:1 in some theatres of operations. In Burma, by improvement in malaria discipline and with the advent of DDT, the ratio of sick to wounded dropped from 120:1 in 1943 to less than 20:1 in 1944.
2. F.A.E. Crew, FRS (ed.) *The Army Medical Services* (HMSO, 1955).
3. The National Archives War Office Records, WO 235/1107. Evidence given by Mrs Fidoe and Miss Williams at the war crimes trial of Lieutenant-General Ito Takeo of the Japanese army, January 1948.
4. Ibid.
5. H. Frei, *The Guns of February: Ordinary Japanese Soldiers' Views of the Malayan Campaign and the Fall of Singapore* (Singapore University Press, 2004), p. 121.
6. L. Warner & J. Sandilands, *Women Behind the Wire* (1982), p. 6.

4

The Fall of Singapore

By the end of January 1942 Hong Kong, Manila and much of Malaya was in Japanese hands. Yet in Singapore's Raffles hotel the New Year had been celebrated in style as usual. Women bejewelled and dressed in all their finery, and men with their dinner jackets, danced the night away and drank champagne as though nothing untoward was happening. In some respects this could be seen as a deliberate act of defiance, but it could also be argued that it was the British stiff upper lip attitude gone mad. At this stage there was no talk of evacuating civilians or military personnel to places of greater safety. Indeed, General Percival, who had taken over the command of Malaya in May 1941, seemed to be in an extremely defiant mood, although in fairness this was perhaps dictated by the thought that reinforcements were possibly on their way to the island.

British propaganda continued to refer to the island of Singapore as an impregnable fortress and it appears that for a considerable time military personnel believed this rhetoric. Even when the two crucial British battleships in the area, the *Repulse* and the *Prince of Wales*, were sunk by the Japanese in December 1941, officers continued to maintain that Singapore was a bastion of the British Empire that could not be invaded. These battleships had been sent specifically to protect the island, and since there was very little in the way of air cover, their loss was a devastating blow to British defence strategy. Newspaper journalists tried to rally groups together and encourage an exodus from Keppel harbour, but the seriousness of the situation did not appear to have penetrated the general public. General Percival, meanwhile, was clearly concerned about the intelligence reports he had received from Hong Kong but chose to wait for the time being and rally his troops.

Margot, who was an extremely intelligent person, was not in the least bit fooled by blustering propaganda. She had discussed the war situation and the Japanese threat with her friend Kiwi on many occasions and they were both aware of the imminent danger. Increasing battle sounds also signalled the need to be on high alert. Then orders were received on Christmas Eve to move the 17th General Hospital backwards because battles were nearing Tanjong and Malim. An ambulance train and some of the staff moved most of the patients and the remaining staff walked along the track later to find another train. They were an unusual sight, since they were also carrying their Christmas dinner in the hope that they could cook it on the train.

Two days later the Japanese bombed and destroyed Tanjong Malim station and there were no further trains. At this point Margot was placed in the Alexandra Hospital, which was 5 miles west of Singapore city. A few days later she was moved yet again to Changi in the extreme north-west of the island. The officers' mess overlooked the Johore Straits, but she had little time to admire the view. Soon after her arrival the air-raid sirens sounded and she and some other nurses leapt into a slit trench for cover; they quickly leapt back out again, however, because the trench was teaming with red ants and leeches. In addition, there were a number of increasingly violent tropical storms to contend with, and at one point it was difficult to describe which sounds were those of an approaching storm and which noises originated from the onslaught of battle. Kiwi in particular found the intensity of the storms terrifying, while Margot found it somewhat easier to distinguish between the possible but unlikely threat that was being posed by nature, and the very real threat of an advancing enemy.

Their task in Changi was to assist the move of patients down to Singapore city. This assignment was extremely difficult as constant air raids and shell attacks hampered all movement. Margot and Kiwi were the last to leave and got caught up in a very heavy shell attack. Both took cover under a large wooden kitchen table and Margot grabbed a bottle of brandy, which hitherto had only been used for medicinal purposes. She later recalled, with some amusement, that the shell attack did not seem anywhere near so fierce once she and Kiwi had taken a few large swigs from the bottle. Their duty was to their patients and all military nurses were amazingly composed under fire. The British Army official medical account of the conflict praised the courage and coolness of nurses in their struggle to put their patients' safety before that of their own:

> At a time when casualties were most numerous, hospital accommodation for them was most scarce, for hospitals were bombed, burnt and destroyed. There was soon no place on the island where the wounded man could be safeguarded from further hurt; no place where he could feel at rest. The surgical team [of which Margot was a member] and the operating theatre shared the hazards of the machine gun and the gun pit; the nursing orderly in the ward was alongside the rifleman in his trench. The congestion was such that the Red Cross could provide no protection, for if [a relief aircraft] flew over a hospital its shadow encroached on a battery site. The piped water supply of the hospitals quickly became utterly insufficient; water had to be carried to the wards in buckets, and in buckets the refuse and excrement had to be carried out. For the patient gravely hurt, there was no healing hope of evacuation; amid the noise of battle he breathed the anxiety and hopelessness that tinctured the air, and waited for the coming horror magnified by his stimulated imagination.[1]

Military nurses were astounding in terms of their bravery and dedication to duty, and much of this was due to the integrity of their individual characters. Disciplined training within the armed forces successfully strengthened their existing resolve in difficult situations. Military psychiatrists had long argued that certain characteristics and early influences made some people less susceptible to terror and fear. They had introduced psychometric testing for new recruits following the First World War and understood the key requirements which mentally underpinned successful military strategy.

They recognised, first and foremost, that group camaraderie and loyalty was crucial in terms of keeping a cool, rational mind in the midst of chaos. Faith in military leadership was also essential in order to instil confidence in certain decisions and courses of action. As official military guidelines propounded:

> The officer (male or female) in combat situations occupies a place that to his men is close to godhead. The officer's leadership influence is central in restraining harmful emotions both in military and civilian contexts.[2]

Margot's military training had cultivated her pre-existing air of authority and natural leadership skills. People gravitated towards her in crisis situations and frequently relied on her level-headed advice. As the bombs rained down on Singapore, Margot remained in control of her own sphere of medical influence. She dutifully followed military orders but also took the initiative when necessary.

On 8 and 9 February there was an intense bombing of the island and radio broadcasts declared that the Japanese forces had landed on the north-west area of Singapore. By the 10th it was clear that these same Japanese forces were taking over the whole island and the British and Australians were powerless to stop them. The Royal Air Force had mounted a last-ditch, desperate, heroic and futile attack against the Japanese, but to no avail. Surprisingly, the British national press announced on 12 February that General Percival still remained defiant:

> British troops are this morning fighting to the end in the shelled and bombed suburbs of Singapore city against tank and tommy-gun infantry onslaughts. Another Japanese note calling on General Percival to surrender has been ignored. News of British defiance was given in a Singapore communiqué which reached London late last night, breaking an official silence of 36 hours. It admitted that the Japanese were driving fiercely on the city, their tanks being supported by bombers and fighters. The surrender demand was made at 7.30 in the morning. According to a Tokyo communiqué, the Japanese at 8 o'clock entered the city 'after breaking desperate resistance.' It added the claim that 'remnants of British troops were being mopped up.' Japan's capital

immediately began celebrating the fall of the city. But later Tokyo radio spoke of 'fierce hand to hand fighting in the streets.'

The Singapore communiqué said: 'The enemy drive from the west has been directed on Singapore city, and has been pressed with vigour during the night. In addition, there has been some infiltration today. The enemy advance has been assisted by considerable bomber and fighter support, and our troops covering the west sector have been forced further back. At 7.30 this morning a Japanese note dropped by air addressed to the High Command asked for the unconditional surrender of our entire forces. No reply has been made to this note. In the western and north western sector bitter fighting continues. In the east of the island enemy activity has been slight.' Tokyo indicated that the Singapore city battle is going on in a sea of flames. The railway station, Keppel Harbour, and several districts in the western sector were reported to be ablaze.[3]

In reality, the Japanese had already conquered the island as soon as their troops had reached the island's reservoirs. Control of the water supply effectively gave them control of the island, since neither the British Army nor the island's 700,000 civilians could last more than a couple of days without water. While the battles raged all around him, General Percival initiated efficient but perhaps rather belated evacuation orders. By this time, news of the Japanese atrocities that had been committed against military nursing sisters had reached his ears and he was adamant that all nurses should leave the island forthwith.

Matrons of all military hospitals had asked for nurses to volunteer to leave; none of them did so, such was their devotion to duty and their patients. Matrons were thus required to choose which nurses should leave and which should stay – in some cases names were simply picked out of a hat. The first group of nurses left the island on 11 February, bound for Batavia on a ship named *Empire Star*. This vessel arrived safely at its destination and then proceeded to India. The following day, Margot's officers' mess was bombed by the Japanese and she was almost hit by an exploding shell. Although throughout the intense bombardment she had remained outwardly stoical and calm, she felt considerably shaken by such a close call. Moreover, by this stage even the most ludicrously optimistic British officer could deduce that the writing was already on the wall for Singapore. As land battles continued to rage and air attacks became more frequent, British Rear Admiral Spooner issued an order that all remaining sea vessels should leave Keppel harbour and set a course for Java.

Margot was thus evacuated at long last, with fifty other nursing sisters and four matrons. Under heavy gunfire, they were all escorted to a small ship called *Kuala*, which was already heaving under the pressure of 400 women and children and 300 officers.

The *Kuala* and another ship, *Tien Kwang*, set sail at 7 p.m. By this time Singapore was totally ablaze, and oil and petrol tanks were systematically destroyed by the British forces in order to prevent these resources from falling into Japanese hands. Throughout the night the *Kuala* and *Tien Kwang* made very slow progress and the latter had developed engine problems by dawn. At 8 a.m. a Japanese plane spotted both ships; it circled for a while before soaring upwards and into the distance. Everyone heaved a collective sigh of relief, believing that the danger was over.

At midday, however, the plane returned and bombed both ships near the island of Pom Pong. The *Kuala* received a direct hit. Three matrons who were sitting at a table below deck were killed instantly by the explosion, and the other was viciously machine-gunned in the water as she desperately tried to swim to safety. As the *Kuala* rapidly sank deeper into the sea, Margot managed to escape the deck amid the frantic scramble for survival. She vigorously kicked off her shoes and jumped. Once in the water she swam with all her might, diving deeply under the water each time the Japanese planes came over. A man trying to help her had kindly taken off her tin hat as soon as she had hit the water. After a lot of determined effort, and dodging of machine-gun fire, Margot and some other survivors reached the relative safety of the nearby island of Pom Pong. Here they made makeshift beds out of grass and leaves and organised a shift rota to take care of the wounded and gather fuel for a night-time fire. They scoured the island looking for possible fresh water supplies and sources of food. A few days later they were picked up by a small trading ship called the *Tanjong Penang*, which set sail early in the morning on 17 February 1942.

Their journey was cut short, however, by yet another Japanese attack. Margot recalled the sequence of events:

When the Japs were coming down the hospitals were eventually evacuated to Singapore. Then when things got really bad General Percival decided that families and nurses had to go. He had heard what was happening in Hong Kong. People have often queried why we nursing sisters left but we were ordered to go. We all had to go. I eventually left on Friday 13th, we were ordered to go; we didn't want to leave. We had to do as we were told. The ship sailed that night and a lot of people were bombed and killed before we even left the harbour. Then the next morning we were apparently next to a ship that held key personnel. The ship wasn't working so we were anchored off a small island called Pom Pong. Some people had gone ashore to get camouflage to try and camouflage the ship. Reconnaissance planes came over and saw us. Then later on they came back and bombed us. Our ship got a direct hit. A lot of people were killed. I was in the water swimming about, but there were strong currents and people were taken to various islands, you didn't see them again.

Anyway, there were a lot of nurses on this island and a lot of wounded. They managed to get some medical supplies off the other ship before that was bombed again the next day. We divided ourselves into shifts to nurse the wounded and I happened to be off duty when a ship came in on the Monday night, and the captain said that he would take the sick but not the women and children, and he wanted some nurses. Those who were off duty went, and of course everyone thought that we were getting away and … they were being left behind. We didn't know where we were going, but I presumed Java. All that day we helped with the sick.

It was a little tiny boat with about three hundred people on board, it probably only held about fifty or twenty normally. At any rate, we got a light flashed on us and I think we were shelled and the ship went down in about five minutes with everybody on board. I again found myself in the water, and with another QA, who I didn't know at the time was badly wounded, we managed to tie two rafts together and collect sixteen people. There was just room for someone to sit on a raft and hold a baby, but gradually people drifted away, what with the sun and one thing and another. In the end I was left with one other lady. We were just sitting back to back and we would paddle with our hands because we could see land, but the currents were so queer there. At any rate, she had this little bit of wood and that went and she went with it and I was left alone. I was by myself then for a day and a night, which was the fourth night I think.[4]

By this stage Margot no longer had the strength to rescue anyone because she was barely hanging on to the threads of her own life:

> Mrs Barnett let the paddle slip from her grasp and, before I could stop her, she had plunged into the sea after it, clutching the two life jackets with her as she went. I was much too weak to swim after her. I called and strained my eyes to catch sight of her − but there was just nothing. I was now all alone. It was at this moment that I became acutely conscious of the will to live. I was determined to hold on to life as long as it was humanly possible. I prayed that help would come and felt very definitely that some unseen power was watching over me. Why me, and not those others who had drifted away? I managed to catch a few drops of rainwater in the lid of my powder compact and also ate some seaweed that drifted near the raft. Night came and I watched the stars and soaked up the rain that fell on me. I thought of home and my family and the happy things in my life.[5]

During her time on the raft Margot committed the dead bodies, one by one, to the cruel Java Sea. The last of these was a small baby that had given up the fight against the searing heat and intense dehydration. The QA that had helped her construct the raft, Sister Le Blanc-Smith, was severely wounded and also died. Being adrift on the Java Sea was an extremely lonely and frightening experience, since the deep waters, with their peculiar undercurrents, contained numerous sharks, as Margot grimly recalled:

> There were plenty of sharks around, but of course they had got so much to eat. There were so many ships that had been sunk during that week. Then I saw a great ship coming [laughs quietly], I didn't know what it was, but it happened to be a Japanese ship, and I, of course, was burnt black by the sun, and they probably thought that I was Malay. They picked me up. Someone came down and tied a rope around my waist and hauled me over the top. I had drunk rainwater that I caught in my powder compact

and eaten some seaweed. I probably could have gone on for a bit, but they gave me a change of clothes and put a rug down. There was a doctor on board who had trained in America and he didn't let me have too much to drink, because all I wanted to do was drink. Of course my legs also seemed to have gone, because when we eventually put into a port and they said we were getting off the ship, I couldn't walk, because my legs wouldn't work. But then they discovered later that I had some sea water boils when I was taken to this camp.

On board the ship they gave me some milk, even a tot of whisky or brandy or something like that. The doctor was very good, but like he said, he was a doctor not a soldier. Then we got to Muntok, which was an island about sixty miles down river. The pier was very long and there were British troops, who, I hadn't realised then, were working for the Japanese. I just heard these voices and they were absolutely wonderful, and they asked me if I'd like anything. They had tins of fruit and offered them to me, I said 'Oh yes that would be lovely', so they gave me some fruit but I couldn't eat it. I eventually ended up in what I think was a Chinese jail. There were civilian men and a lot of women, children and army personnel. The Japs were gathering everyone there and then in a week or so we were split up, so that's how I became a prisoner.[6]

Margot's survival experience on the raft was miraculous and there were many times when she felt as though she could not go on. Catching rainwater and eating seaweed undoubtedly helped her to maintain her physical strength, but it was her indomitable mental, emotional and spiritual strength that pulled her through this extraordinarily difficult time. Margot later stated that during her time on the raft she thought continually of happier times that she had spent with friends and family.

She prayed to God intensely, frequently and fervently, and refused to let despair overwhelm her. She remembered that during her nurse training one of her tutors had emphasised the importance of a strong mind in terms of keeping the body healthy. In later years, she laughingly recalled that this tutor had always claimed that a healthy strong mind dictated subconscious instructions to the body to promote healthy living. Margot firmly believed, therefore, that during her time on the raft, having the strong will to live had undoubtedly been her most important survival tool. But by the time she was hauled up onto the decks of the Japanese battleship she had very little strength left, and she acknowledged that it was unlikely that she could have held out for much longer.

Eventually the Japanese battleship docked in Muntok harbour on the Dutch East Indies island of Banka, just off the coast of Sumatra. By this time the Japanese had discovered that, despite appearances to the contrary, Margot was not Malay and they bombarded her with questions:

> They kept asking me where I was going when I was on the boat and I said that I didn't know where the boat was headed, this was the truth. They also asked me where I'd come from. Conditions in the jail were terrible, and of course at this time I was rather sick. These red patches had come up on my legs and nobody knew what they were. They were actually deep-seated boils, and if nothing had been done I could have got septicaemia and died; but there was a wonderful Scottish doctor who said that he'd got a blunt scalpel and he incised them and let all the bad stuff out and I sort of turned the corner then. But it was just overcrowded and there was no room to do anything and very little food. Everybody didn't quite know what had hit them.[7]

Back in Singapore the British surrender was signed by General Percival on 15 February and hostilities ceased at 8.30 p.m. that evening. The Japanese celebrated with a parade of triumph and raised the Japanese flag high above the golf courses, cricket pavilions and Government House. Eighty-five thousand British, Australian and Indian troops were now Japanese prisoners of war. Japanese soldiers imposed a colour bar and separated Indian troops from the rest. They were taken to Farrar park camp and some were persuaded to enlist in the Indian National Army, since Japanese armed forces were supposedly planning to help Indian nationals liberate their country from British colonial rule. The captured Australian and British troops were initially taken to Changi barracks and then to the river valley camps. Many of them were later used to build what became known as the 'railway of death', the military supply line which ran between Siam and Burma.

Once prisoners of war had been dispatched, Japanese soldiers and military police turned their attention to Singapore's Chinese population. According to official records, there were 700,000 Chinese men, women and children living and working in Singapore when the Japanese invaded. Many of these were subsequently massacred. Targeted as displaying anti-Japanese thoughts and tendencies, the Chinese were 'screened' over a period of three days; those lucky enough to pass the screening procedure were issued with a good citizen pass. Those who failed the screening tests were executed en mass, on rubber estates, on the sides of roads, in jungles and on beaches. The precise number of innocent victims is not known, but it is estimated that at least 50,000 Chinese people were killed by Japanese soldiers in these ethnic purges.

Prisoners of war were also subjected to extremely sadistic treatment since Japanese ministers had never ratified the Geneva Convention and applied their own highly dubious code of conduct to the supervision of prisoners.

For Margot and other bedraggled survivors of the numerous shipwrecks that littered the Java Sea, the misery of Muntok pier was combined with an overwhelming sense of numbed shock as they adjusted to their dramatically changed circumstances. Among the women and children herded together on the pier there was a mixture of nationalities, a mixture of cultures and languages, and a mixture of social classes. Dazed and debilitated, they tried to recount the details of their capture and subsequent treatment. Their world had changed so suddenly and viciously it was difficult for them to comprehend why fate had placed them in such a fraught and terrifying situation. Margot was simply too faint and weak at this point to tell her story to others; she needed all her energy just to hang on to life. In total, Margot spent three weeks in the desperate squalor of Muntok prison before moving first to Charitas Hospital and then Palembang prisoner-of-war camp. For the next three and a half years she was to remain a prisoner of war, interned within a variety of camps and locations, but always at the mercy of the Japanese.

Notes

1. F.A.E. Crew, FRS, *The Army Medical Services Campaigns*, Vol. II, HM Stationery Office.
2. The National Archives War Office Records, WO 222/218. *Morale, Discipline and Mental Fitness* (1940), p. 4.
3. *Daily Express* front page, 12 February 1942.
4. Imperial War Museum Oral History Interview with Dame Margot Turner, ref. 9196.
5. J. Smyth, *The Will to Live* (1970).
6. IWM Oral History Interview with Dame Margot Turner, ref. 9196.
7. Ibid.

5

Palembang

The confusion and misery of Muntok pier intensified during the latter weeks of February and early March 1942. Singapore was now fully occupied by enemy forces and the rising sun flags of the Japanese continued to be ceremonially hoisted above old British-controlled territories and littered the once perfectly landscaped gardens and government buildings. The dignified European women who, up until a few weeks previously, had been buying silk stockings during their morning shopping sprees, enjoying sedate afternoon teas, early evening cocktails and late-night dinner dances, were uncomfortably and suddenly confronted with Japanese soldiers urinating on their terraces, pushing them sharply in their backs with rifle butts and rough handling them towards internment camps. They were firmly herded, along with several other groups of survivors, to what used to be a clearing station for native coolie labour. From here they were taken and housed in a huge gloomy warehouse that had previously been used as a prison, but in more recent times was a convenient storage centre for pepper and other spices.

The coolie barracks consisted of a number of hutted dormitories, each containing a series of sloping concrete slabs. They had formally housed around twenty coolies in each dormitory. In previous times these coolies had worked long, tiring hours in the Dutch tin mines. There was a narrow passageway between each concrete slab, and the women did their best to sort out their meagre belongings into some sort of order. But as night fell and the women tried tenaciously to sleep on the slabs, they slid further and further towards the floor as the night wore on. The noisy tin roof leaked in several places and the only toilet facilities consisted of a foul-smelling drain at the back of the building, where people simply squatted to answer their calls of nature, in full view of anyone passing by. Since many of the inhabitants eventually succumbed to dysentery, the stench of the over-filled, putrid drain wafted across the barracks and covered the huts like some evil miasma.

Washing facilities were very basic. Women crammed alongside the native tong, which looked like an oversized, oblong, trench bath, and resembled the kind of animal trough that some farmers used to feed their cattle. There was no privacy of any kind. Water supplies were tainted, because some prisoners had already washed their dirty laundry in the same water, and the water had often been used by bathers. Bored and curious Japanese guards often queued up to observe the women at the tong. Amongst these beleaguered women were those who had hitherto soaked in luxurious baths, surrounded by servants who eagerly answered their calls and attended to their every whim. Now they were reduced to scooping up pathetically small amounts of murky water in tin cans and throwing it over their weary bodies in an attempt to maintain some semblance of hygiene.

The men, women and children were a mixture of races but generally they fell into one of the following groups: Europeans, Chinese, Asiatic and Eurasian. Men were kept in a separate quarter and, later, in a separate camp. Margot recalled the rampant xenophobia of the different racial groups, the desperately cramped accommodation and the constant whimpering of babies and small children. For her part, Margot, with her painful, deep sea boils, black skin and severely dehydrated body, was accommodated and nursed among the sick and wounded. As the prisoners of Muntok grew substantially in number, the Japanese gradually shifted groups to Palembang in Sumatra, which was about 60 miles up the Moesi River. Margot was moved by stretcher on 1 April 1942 and continued to be nursed by some Dutch nuns for about a month. She recalled:

After about two or three weeks they took the civilian men to a Palembang camp and the service men to another camp, and we went to Palembang. First of all we were in Dutch houses. This was, I suppose, about the beginning of April, and the Dutch, of course, had just caved in. They had got these houses that would normally house four people now housing about sixteen or twenty. You just slept on the floor, and in those early days they used to bring rations in. We appointed people to be in charge so we had our own camp commandant and a committee. You had to do that when there were so many people, and we had Dutch and British together. We gathered together in groups, about six or eight of us looking after each other. They were friends that you made, and I got in with some nurses. I didn't know anyone when I went into the camp at first. One other QA came into the camp but she unfortunately died. There were quite a few civilian sisters and, of course, Australian sisters, they were with us all the time. There was just a guard at the gate, I mean, we couldn't go anywhere. There was nowhere to go, we didn't speak the language and we would have to go miles down river before getting to the sea. There was no question of ever trying to escape.

There were two or three guards there and they used to come around periodically. We were counted every morning and every evening, so we had to line up outside the houses. They were particularly bad at counting so we often stood for quite a while. Though of course, when one looks back, those early days which seemed pretty awful were really the better days because the civilians were looking after us. I was in that camp until the October, with the British, with my own people. The four of us were taken out to nurse in a native hospital, another QA, myself and two civilian sisters. This was where the other nationalities who weren't interned with us came in. Some were Japanese. But they always said that we could eventually work in the Dutch hospital where there were the sick; and we did nurse in this hospital with two Dutch doctors and a dentist. It was nice to have something to do.[1]

For the first few months Margot was tenderly nursed back to health by the Roman Catholic nuns of the Charitas Order at their long-established hospital. They applied twice daily hot poultices to her deep sea boils and dressed and applied clean bandages to the potential sites of infection. Once recovered, Margot eased her way back into nursing, and between October

1942 and April 1943 Margot worked long hours as a nurse in the native Charitas and Dutch hospitals. By this time Margot had befriended a civilian nurse named Netta Smith. The two of them became very close, partly because they shared a similar sense of humour and partly because they both possessed an indomitable and stoical approach to daily problems. Netta was originally from Aberdeen and was a short, feisty lady who had been working as a nurse in Singapore like many of the other women interned alongside her. She was also a survivor of the *Kuala* and had dived deep into the sea every time a Japanese plane had come over – much the same as Margot had done.

Netta had also had the traumatic experience of watching her best friend die of a shrapnel wound as she sat beside her on the ship's deck, before they had even left the harbour. Following the shipwreck Netta had managed to cling to a wooden box along with a young Eurasian girl, until they were rescued by a small boat. Some of the passengers onboard had already perished and they heaved them into the water. There were about forty survivors in Netta's small craft, some Chinese and some Eurasian. They clung together for warmth and bathed their open wounds in the sea. For three days and nights they had nothing to eat, although at one stage a large bird flew over their boat carrying a big fish. The passengers duly created a huge din and succeeded in getting the bird to drop the fish into the boat; they then divided it into small portions and ate it raw.

By the time Netta was picked up by the Japanese and herded into Palembang there were only thirty survivors left in her group. She recalled amusingly that her only white uniform was in tatters and she had one bra and one pair of knickers to her name, not even a handbag. Upon her arrival at the camp she struck up an almost immediate affinity with Margot, and the women were mutually supportive of each other from the outset. Each day, on finishing their nursing work, they would return to the camp to complete their camp chores. Each prisoner had set tasks allotted to them, and the all-female community constructed a working environment that attempted to offer mutual support to all internees. In part because of her large frame, Margot was put in charge of the wood-cutting squad, and she and her team were henceforth responsible for chopping, sawing and collecting all the wood for night fires. The work was physically hard but the mischievous Margot always managed to create laughter amongst her fellow prisoners:

We used to tease the Japanese. We used to have great laughs at their expense. They didn't know what we were laughing about at times. We used to make them do things. For instance, sawing a tree, we used to say that there was something wrong with the saw you see, and we'd make heavy weather of it. There was nothing wrong at all, but they'd come along and see, and they'd do it and say 'there is nothing wrong you see.' But then they'd done this bit of sawing of this big tree for us, you see. We knew there was nothing wrong. We often baited the Japanese. We used to try and laugh at the Japanese all the time but they never knew that we were laughing at them.[2]

Humorous episodes such as these helped to maintain camp morale, but on 6 April 1943 Margot's internment took a sinister turn:

Suddenly they [the Japanese guards] sent for us one day and we were told that this was something to do with our passes, but it wasn't, so we sat and waited. There was this Dutch doctor and his wife and he was something to do with the Red Cross and eventually we were interviewed, not by the civilians but by the Kempeitai, which were like the Gestapo. They beat the doctor and his wife up and then told the doctor, myself and [the] other QA to go, but they kept the others. We didn't know what happened to them. We went back to the hospital and the doctor said to me, 'its best that you go back to camp, because I have got to go back tomorrow and I am not coming back, I know.' I asked to speak to the Japanese about going back and explained what had happened. We'd heard in the meantime that the others were in the local jail. One of the Malay police had told us this the night before.

Anyway, they collected us and we got a few little things. Patients would give us things like a small packet of oatmeal and we always kept it, because we'd think, well we might need that. We'd put it away in a bag we'd made out of sacking. Anyway, they came to collect us and we thought 'Oh good, we're going', and then they stopped by the jail. We thought, 'Oh are they going to collect the others?' We thought we were going back to our own people but not a bit of it! We were bundled out, our possessions were taken from us and they cleared two people out of a cell and put us in. We went into this cell in this jail. To this day we do not know what we did wrong. We are still waiting to hear!

They said something about the black out I think, first of all. But we were so conscious of the black out, I mean, having the war in Malaya and one thing and another. We didn't even light up a cigarette at night if we had one. In the houses we didn't have any lights. We knew nothing really. We were separated two and two and we didn't meet up again for three months. Then we were allowed to walk between the walls. After a while we were just sent for again. They were bringing a lot of people in and there were a lot of horrible things going on in the jail, and after six months we were sent for to go back to the camp. We were told that if we committed the same crime again then we would go back in for years. But since we didn't know what crime we were supposed to have committed in the first place it was a bit pointless to warn us not to commit the same crime![3]

The majority of prisoners in Palembang jail were murderers and thieves. But regardless of what crime these fellow prisoners had committed, they treated Margot with respect and a level of affection. It was also a centre for sadistic torture techniques and horrendous cruelty. Margot would not be drawn on that period of her life, other than to state in a very subdued voice:

The other prisoners were a rum lot, I don't know what they had done but they were good to me. They shared their food if they had any and they were considerate. There were so many unspeakable things going on. It is not something that I really talk about much – the things they were doing to local people. You could hear the screams. There are some things that were unspeakable – even in the books that are written about it. I don't say anything about it. It is just something I don't say.[4]

Following a period of six months, some lengthy interrogations and brutal treatment the Japanese prison guards eventually announced that Margot was to be released. On 22 October 1943, the day that Margot was released from Palembang jail, her fellow inmates back at the camp were in the process of moving location:

They were moving from the houses to the men's camp. The men had not realised that the women were going in there – [Margot laughs quietly] and they had left it in a filthy state. I am sure they would not have left it like that if they had known.[5]

The men's camp had been built on swampy ground and diseases such as typhoid and dysentery were rife. For some women, the constant and often appalling struggle for survival overwhelmed them and they simply 'turned their faces to the wall' and died. The more robust women prisoners of war had coined this latter phrase in the early months of their internment to describe those who had died as a direct result of losing all semblance of hope. The phrase epitomised those women who had given up in spirit and gradually lost the will to live. Many of them had been consumed with despair after being separated from their husbands, fiancés and sons. Often the Japanese guards would issue information about the men folk and list those that had died in the other camps, but they would never tell the women concerned straight away. Instead, they would hint at their demise and play mind games until the women gave up all hope of ever being reconciled with their loved ones.

Those women who remained helplessly watched their numbers diminish. They guarded their friends' bodies overnight in the sheltered, raised hut that was designed for just such a purpose; they prayed for their souls and dug their graves. Often the only difference that could be discerned between those who survived and those who died was their mental resilience. Mental attitude was imperative in the camps and a positive approach was seen as the saviour of all.

In addition to the poor-quality, rationed food, hard work, routine and frequent hut inspections, physical deprivations, disease, lack of water and annoying malarial-carrying mosquitoes, one of the most irritating and frustrating aspects of being in the camp was the impromptu and often tedious 'Tenkos'. All women were required to bow very low every time they were confronted with a Japanese guard as a mark of respect to their persecutors, but they also had to rally in the prison yard whenever the guard shouted 'Tenko'. The literal meaning of *tenko* is simply 'roll call', and the guards were required to count and record the number of prisoners that were present at each occasion. All prisoners were instructed to bow very low yet again during these roll calls, and to keep their bodies bowed throughout the counting process until they were dismissed. Women would attempt to cheer each other up by saying that the process of bowing from the waist during Tenkos at least kept their figure exercised. At this stage the women were supervised by Japanese and Indonesian civilians and some, Margot maintained, were not adequately equipped for the task:

The Japanese that were looking after us were the lowliest of the lowliest. They had probably been coolies or something before the war, and to have white women as prisoners, they thought this was something – they were lording it over us. We had to do what they told us to do. But on the whole they were a very poor type, the guards were a very poor type. They were Japanese with a few Koreans but mostly Japanese, and tiny of course. Some of them were human I think, in that they wanted to talk about their families. They might have felt sorry for us, I don't know, but most didn't. We were a very mixed bunch and I think that some of the women may have had some personal contact with the guards, but as far as most of us were concerned they [the guards] were anonymous. You just made your friends amongst the people you lived with. The guards did not always mistreat us but we were punished if we did something they did not like. Tenkos often took quite a long time because the guards were not very good at counting.

One day we were standing there being counted and I thought, 'I am in the British Army, I am a QA, an officer, a British Army nurse. I am not Japanese', and I did not stand to attention or bow, and I got a fist in my face which knocked a tooth out. So I learnt my lesson the hard way. If you did something they did not agree with then you had to stand out in the sun. When the women died we all dug graves, and we made about three cemeteries all told, I think.[6]

Margot's defiance and rebellious stance was partly inspired by the knowledge that she was, in fact, a commissioned officer. All registered nurses in the British armed forces were awarded official commissioned officer status in 1941, as a result of a campaign initiated by the matron-in-chief of the army, Dame Katherine Jones. The latter had been moving her nurses ever forward onto the front line in a bid to get this status for her nurses, and she was delighted when her efforts were successful. Officer status gave due recognition and value to military nurses and also had repercussions for the civilian nursing service in terms of raising status. By assimilating to the army pattern, military nurses became an integral part of the army framework and their position was assured in terms of pay and promotion prospects. But it was also believed by some at the War Office that giving registered nurses officer status would offer them some protection against maltreatment should they fall into enemy hands. The atrocities that were committed against military nurses in Hong Kong, however, had already demonstrated that this was not the case. The only way for nurses to escape sexual attention, and the dire consequences this could bring, was to adopt more devious methods. Thus nurses and other women in the prison camps did their utmost to repel Japanese attention by altering their appearance and trying to make themselves look as ugly as possible:

> In the early days the Japanese tried to get some ---- they tried to get some Australian nurses to go to a nightclub, but of course they just dressed themselves up in all sorts of things, and put mud on their faces to make them look very unattractive, so they reckoned that there was not going to be [any sexual favours] there. There was also a black market going on, but I had no money and nothing to sell.[7]

Some women also became adept at making rashes, huge pimples or make-believe scars on their skin to fake contagious illness, which was guaranteed to ward off any unwanted attention. But generally women were left to their own devices as long as they pulled their weight on the work front and remembered to bow low to the Japanese guards whenever they encountered them walking across the camp or entering their huts, and during the interminable Tenkos. After the initial shock at their dramatic change in circumstances, most women rallied around each other and established a very powerful and effective sisterhood in the face of their common enemy. Their old way of life was gradually forgotten and replaced by a daily struggle for survival. Moreover, the women very quickly recognised that they were in this struggle together and each needed to depend on the other in ways that would have been totally unthinkable before their captivity. Without their men, their fathers, husbands and brothers, women were forced to fend for themselves and gain strength from each other. In terms of resourcefulness, innovation and courage, many became pleasantly surprised by how well they adapted and rose to the challenge that confronted them. One woman noted:

> Before camp I had led a very sheltered, privileged life. In camp there was no privacy. You couldn't go into a room and shut the door. I mixed with all sorts of people and it made me understand them and feel in the future that I could mix with everybody. I was so much more trusting of human nature than when I went in.[8]

Another claimed:

> You could be eccentric if you wanted to be and nobody commented. A lot of us did what I suppose would now be called off beat things. You were free to indulge in whatever it was that you wanted to pursue that in some way expressed yourself. Not before or since have I lived a life as rich. You could be exactly who you were – find yourself, I would say. Once we came out we were less free.[9]

This sentiment was a recurring theme in camp survivors:

> Funnily enough, camp life was an extremely rich period. Yesterday had happened, tomorrow might never come, so you lived for the day and the people who were there. There were no other encumbrances whatsoever.

> I grew up in those camps. I came out of myself and realised my strengths. I shall always be grateful for those years. It was the best school there could ever have been.

Because we had no men to help us it was only our strength and nobody else's. I learnt that women can be very brave, very tenacious. If it had not been for that I would not be here now.

Before the war I hadn't been too keen on women's company. I came away from the camps liking women and respecting their resource.[10]

Indeed, day-to-day life in the camps was, in some respects, a wonder to behold, since it constantly revealed the astonishing resourcefulness of women prisoners. Despite the alien environment and tropical climate, which included the pungent smells of the jungle, the prickly and unrelenting heat of the searing sun, periods of torrential rainfall and disease-ridden swamps, thriving communities were built from scratch. Schools, hospitals, social clubs and religious concerts were all planned, constructed and organised by women. Amidst the profusion of bamboo, rubber and palm trees, tropical flowers of all colours and descriptions, impenetrable jungle territory, and surrounded on all sides by thick, foliage-covered streams, creeks, rivers and the ever-present barbed-wire fence, the women painstakingly built their new lives. In defiance of their captors, they became determined not to live an overly passive, docile and compliant existence. Like a mythical phoenix emerging from the ashes, a new sense of kinship developed. Daily routines, food gathering and sharing, cooking, cleaning, building, engineering, plumbing, designing, the black market trade, child care and mutual protection frameworks were all devised, implemented and maintained by the remarkable and resourceful female prisoners of Sumatra.

Notes

1. Imperial War Museum Oral History Interview with Dame Margot Turner, ref. 9196.
2. Ibid.
3. Ibid.
4. Ibid.

5. Ibid.
6. Ibid.
7. Ibid.
8. L. Warner & J. Sandilands, *Women Behind the Wire* (1982), p. 5.
9. Ibid.
10. Ibid.

6

Chinese Cabbage and Kang Kong

For the most part, the daily life in Margot's internment camp, like many others of its kind, centred on basic survival needs. During the early months of internment the Dutch were the most fortunate of prisoners, since they had arrived with large stocks of tinned meat and vegetables, milk and a good supply of tea and coffee. Most of the remaining prisoners were the exhausted, bedraggled survivors of a variety of shipwrecks, and terrified women and children who were captured as they fled from their homes under the onslaught of Japanese bombs. Extra rations of food could be obtained by entering the black market trade, but as Margot recalled:

The Dutch had just caved in of course when the Japanese invaded. But the Dutch weren't on ships. They were taken from their houses and allowed to take a number of suitcases with them to camp. The Dutch were therefore well stocked with clothes and foodstuffs to begin with. They even had some jewellery that cushioned them for a while because they could trade it on the black market. We were all aware that there was a black market going on; and you could get into terrible trouble if you were caught, but it didn't really affect me because I had nothing to sell. I went into the camp in what I stood up in. I found a trunk with policeman's clothes in and made a pair of shorts. Luckily you didn't need many clothes because it was very hot and humid in the day, but it could be very cold at night.[1]

Normal camp rations consisted of rotten vegetables that were delivered by a truck and tipped into the road every morning. Chinese cabbage and kang kong made up the bulk of the meagre rations. The latter was similar to water spinach and grew in the filthy puddles of Palembang; it was also responsible for many cases of dysentery. Each morning the stench of the vegetable wagon signalled the arrival of the women's daily sustenance, and they were escorted under guard into the road to gather up the foul-smelling mixture. The road outside the camp gates effectively became the distribution point for all rations, and despite the repulsive nature of the food on offer, several arguments were prone to break out over the fairness of portion size. Sacks of rice were delivered in much the same way but great care was needed to sift the rice. The sacks frequently contained dirt, weevils and shards of broken glass. For Margot, this diet was particularly loathsome because she had never liked rice, even as a child:

I was given a little bit of rice when I arrived in the camp. It was my first bowl. I told them 'I don't eat rice', and they said, 'You'd better, because it's all you're going to get. We had one bowl a day and some rotten vegetables. Once we had a monkey and quite a few wouldn't eat it so we got a bit extra. It was important to get green stuff for vitamins and we managed to grow some spinach in the compound from the rotten vegetables. We knew there were Red Cross parcels but it was months before we got anything. They said we'd get them if we were good, but I don't know what we were supposed to do to be good. Eventually we got one lot, but they had been pilfered. We got one lump of sugar each and a square of chocolate, but we should have got much more than that. We did manage to chop the roots off some of the rotten vegetables and grow our own fresh vegetables. Some of the roots did not take at all, but we did manage to grow quite a bit of spinach for a while.

They sent us out of the camp one day with some natives to pick some green plants. We always needed to get some green stuff for the vitamins you see, but only the natives knew which plants were safe to eat. Sometimes the guards would come and take one or two people away from the camp. They took a Mother Superior away one day and we didn't know what had happened to her for ages, but she did survive.

The Japanese guards were always fond of shouting 'Japanese very good, British no good, no good!' One sometimes forgets some of the things that went on, and sometimes you just didn't know what was happening in other areas of the camp. There were about six hundred of us and we only really got to know those that were in our section. Apparently someone managed to get a letter out of the camp through somebody who was Chinese, but I didn't know anything about that until afterwards. If people were doing that sort of thing they had to keep it very secret. There were so many things going on that you just never got to know about. It was best to take things as they came, from day to day, and concentrate on getting the food and doing your work. There was plenty of wood around so we were never short of wood for fires and cooking. We just had to meet things from day to day. When you finished your work you just wanted to go to bed. I always had to be doing something and we didn't really have much leisure time.[2]

A new sport took hold of the prisoners on some days. The lack of protein in their everyday diet prompted them to pounce on and attack the native wildlife at any opportunity and they became adept at killing snakes, grasshoppers and skunks. Apparently the latter had a very strong, bitter taste and overpowering aroma when cooked, while the snakes tasted of very salty fish. Grasshoppers had very little taste but the women fried them in the palm oil that was designated for their heating and used their imagination. Evidently their crunchy texture reminded some of the women of prawns and they were thus imagined to be part of a restaurant starter! Hunger was so acute at times, however, that some women suffered severe fainting spells, repeated dizziness and, occasionally, hallucinations.

The international Red Cross delivered aid on a regular basis, but this was rarely seen by the prisoners. Red Cross food parcels were usually stolen by the guards for their own personal use, although some of the food was used to feed their soldiers and the native civilian population. The American naval blockade had made its presence felt as early as mid-1942 and Japan suffered chronic food shortages as a result. American submarines ambushed food convoys en route to Japan and the occupied islands, including Sumatra. Civilians working in the city factories consequently developed the habit of foraging in the countryside every Sunday. They searched for the edible roots of lilies, mulberries and snakes. On one Sunday it was estimated that 900,000 inhabitants of Tokyo abandoned the city in search of food. Inflation had pushed the price of staple foods such as rice and soya beans through the roof, and malnutrition began to affect the nation's health. Those who had not been commandeered for military service were forced to work in the factories for at least sixty hours a week, and the fall in food intake was accompanied by a fall in industrial production. On the outskirts of Tokyo over 25 per cent of civilian workers suffered from chronic dysentery and beriberi.

Since the Japanese government, headed by Prime Minister General Hideki Tojo, were struggling to feed their own military forces and citizens, the obligation to feed their prisoners of war naturally slipped to the bottom of their list of wartime priorities. Thus, as the war progressed the prisoners' rations were drastically reduced and all of the women, except for those who were incapacitated by disease, were forced to dig up the whole prison compound to plant food. Occasionally the women were given a banana for each prison quarter, and this would be cut up into at least eight pieces to ensure that every woman received some part of the fruit. The banana skins were also fried and eaten. Every last bit of nourishment was extracted from every obtainable food source, although the women were unanimous in stating that fried banana skins actually had the most disgusting taste.

Coping with food shortages and rationing was a deprivation that clearly affected the health of the prisoners, but evidence suggested that those who began camp life on the meagre rations provided actually fared better than those who had been cushioned by extra food items at the start of their period of captivity. Therefore, when food became increasingly scarce it was the Dutch who suffered the most and their mortality rates rose dramatically. As Margot recalled, their constitutions were totally unprepared for the dramatic changes in food supply:

They suffered in the end because while we were on rations from the very beginning they were able to supplement their rations. When they were no longer able to do this because their extra food ran out they missed this very much, so they became sick and quite a few didn't survive. Quite a lot of people felt that they couldn't cope, but you just had to encourage them. But as far as I know, there were no suicides – not to my knowledge at any rate.[3]

On one occasion Margot was fortunate enough to supplement the rotten vegetable ration with protein, by an extraordinary stroke of luck. Within the dusty, enclosed compound the women were housed in a series of huts surrounded by a barbed-wire fence that circled the whole area and only stopped by the huge wooden gates. The guards' houses were situated just outside the main prison compound and many of the guards kept a few chickens in order to eat and sell their eggs. One hot and humid afternoon a cockerel flew over the compound walls and an alert, athletic Margot quickly caught the bird and hurried into her hut with it. The wily bird apparently put up such a spirited fight, with much squawking and pecking, that it initially managed to escape Margot's clutches and fluttered under the bed boards. As the bird, having achieved a temporary reprieve, lay quietly under the bed, there was much heated discussion amongst the others in the hut about whether or not the bird should be kept, and indeed, more importantly, whether or not the Japanese guards would notice its absence. Margot, however, acted decisively as soon as the bird began to stir again, and with a swift arm action she caught the cockerel, wrung its neck with her bare hands and put it in the cooking pot whilst the others were still pontificating over its fate. She recalled the event with some amusement:

It had obviously come from one of the nearby Japanese houses. There was one mad rush to see who could catch it. The poor creature was obviously terrified and made rather a lot of noise. We were afraid that the guard would hear and wonder what was happening. We were terrified the Japanese would find it. It just flew over the camp you see. After a great struggle I eventually caught it, and it was killed, plucked and in the pot in a matter of minutes. Again we hoped that the guard would not do a round and look in the cooking pot, as he often did. Luck was with us, and that evening about sixteen people had a very small taste of chicken. We often wondered whether the Japs missed their cockerel.

Most of our cooking was done in old tins, and it was a sad day for us if any of them sprang a leak. But if one got anything extra like some fruit or eggs and such it was a rule that it went to the hospital or the children. They got a bit extra. We were always hungry and we all lost weight of course. We just had bits of rice and all the hard work. Then we'd get blown out. I was very bloated – not Beri Beri, but some of the rice bloated us. A lot of them died of starvation. I was nine and a half stone before I went in the camp and about six stone when I came home. Even now I hate to see food wasted and I always say that if you are really hungry you will eat anything. We had to survive on what we were given.[4]

The altruistic nature of many of the camp's inhabitants was perhaps one of the most amazing features of camp life. Extra food, however obtained, was always given to the most vulnerable, and the Dutch women were renowned for being very generous with their food and other possessions during the early stages of internment. Much of the camp routine centred on food production, collection and distribution. The remainder was given up pandering to the whims of the Japanese guards. Work began at 6 a.m., when Margot, who was in charge of the wood-cutting squad, began sawing and collecting wood for the cooking fires; the others chopped smaller chunks of wood into more readily accessible firewood. Then the drains were cleaned of their maggots and other putrid debris, rooms were swept with makeshift brooms and the prisoners assembled at the tong to sluice their bodies with the murky water that was supplied in ever-dwindling amounts. Breakfast consisted of a bowl of poor-quality rice and the rest of the morning was given over to collecting the rations and preparing vegetables for the evening meal.

The women were also expected to collect water for the Japanese guards to have their baths. This was usually done in the heat of the day, as the guards were fond of having afternoon baths to relieve themselves from the heat. The process of collecting water often followed one of the never-ending, and what Margot referred to as irksome, Tenkos. The water was collected from a single tap on a barren hillside on the outskirts of thick jungle territory, and the women trailed to and fro, up and down the hill in the intense heat of the Sumatran sun, not only collecting water for the guards' baths but also for their gardens! This work was exhausting because all water had to be lugged up the hill and the women usually had to make several trips before the guards were satisfied with the quantity of water. The women had been effectively transformed into coolies. For the likes of Margot, however, every outing outside the compound walls offered an opportunity to collect more food. Foraging was an important activity as she explained:

> One day we found some sweet potatoes and ran back to the camp with them. Some of the others dropped their potatoes but a few of us managed to run with them hidden up our blouses. We stuck them under the wooden bed boards. The guards used to search our huts but they didn't look under the boards. We just waited until they had gone and then cooked them very quickly and ate them. We had such meagre rations that we took any opportunity to obtain extra food, even if this involved a bit of a risk.[5]

In addition to her nursing work and camp chores, Margot was given to organising night-time foraging parties in the hope of gaining extra food. Occasionally, roots of vegetables growing in the guards' gardens could be snaffled by tunnelling underneath the barbed wire and grabbing the vegetables from underneath the soil. Margot initiated this process and would identify suitable vegetable plots whilst labouring over her wood-cutting duties. She was caught on one occasion, along with her friend Netta, but although they had to stay out in the sun for a while as punishment, they lived to tell the tale.

The prisoners did gain some dietary respite each year on the emperor's birthday. On this day they were allotted four prawns and a banana for each prisoner, along with a long and stilted lecture from the Japanese guards, who duly informed the inmates that Emperor Hirohito was a divine god who needed to be worshipped and thanked for his benevolence towards them. The extra rations were supposedly indicative of the emperor's divine hospitality.

In terms of obtaining food that was additional to rations on an everyday basis, the prisoners could not rely on the emperor's hospitality, divine or otherwise. In the early stages of captivity a thriving black market provided small extras from time to time, such as an egg or fruit. A lot of women had managed to hide money or jewellery in headscarves or elsewhere about their person – even in their corsets. These items could be exchanged for food and cigarettes. But for those without money or jewellery to use as a bargaining tool, there was no alternative but to work for those who were more affluent. Recognising this state of affairs very quickly, Margot and her nursing friend Netta Smith continually volunteered to do the jobs that nobody else wanted to do: 'Netta and I used to clean the toilets and drains. Some Dutch person didn't want to do it so she paid us to do it.'[6]

The latrines were very basic. They consisted of long, stench-filled drains that were usually full of maggots, rats and a variety of spiders, leeches and dead insects. The seats were simply wooden, often splintered, planks that were perched above the drains. Cleaning them was by far the worst job in the camp. Margot and Netta, however, had no choice; if they wanted to earn money they just had to do whatever they could to obtain funds. For the most disgusting job of cleaning the latrines they were paid the princely sum of 10 dollars a week. Furthermore, there was always a list of unpalatable jobs that needed to be done, and Margot and Netta earned their money the hard way. Plagues of rats and spiders also added to their cleaning problems, but at least they were able to purchase some items on the black market such as cigarettes and bananas. Secret exchanges did become more difficult as the war progressed but, as the diary of a captured army reserve nurse reveals, most camps were supplemented to an extent by these flourishing black markets:

During the last year or so a fair bit of smuggling has been going on at night: jewellery going out under the fence and food such as sugar and small sweet bananas (pisang mas) coming in. Not everyone can smuggle; I think one has to be in with the Indonesian guards. It is a dangerous job, but I have not heard of anyone being caught. I removed my engagement ring from nearly the bottom of a Vaseline jar where, with Dr Lyons' permission, I had been allowed to hide it all this time. One of the women who did smuggle arranged to sell it for me through the fence. She got five hundred guilders for it, and I gave her a quarter of that back for commission. These were not Dutch guilders, but Japanese 'banana money' – only of use in the camp to buy smuggled sugar etc. Of course I gave some of it away and it meant that Marjory and I could now buy a few necessities from people in the camp. For instance, Marjory, being small, was able to buy a pair of boy's shoes which he had grown out of. Later Marjory sold a signet ring (better not to let both rings go at once because there was always the risk that the buyer on the other side would not hand over the money).

We all wear 'trompas': shoes made of wood with a piece of canvas over the toes held on both sides by two nails. Our feet stick in the mud, with the result that the canvas breaks away – most annoying in the dark, on frequent trips to the loos (a two hundred yard sprint – a rice diet is not the best for an undisturbed night!). We are a pretty unattractive lot now. In fact, I believe a visiting Japanese man was heard to say that he had never seen such a lot of ugly women and no wonder after so long on a very poor diet – no vitamin tablets in the camp of course. No dentist, not even any toothpaste, no perms, not even any decent soap or shampoo. We wash our hair in cold water, using the ration of one bar a month of soap which, a Dutch woman told me, is the kind they would not have washed their clothes with in peacetime. Soap is very precious and to be guarded.[7]

Although this particular prisoner was not aware of anyone being caught for smuggling, some people met their deaths as a result of being involved in the black market. Often the people caught were the native Malays and they were killed either by extreme torture or simply tied to a stake in the middle of a prison compound and left to die in the scorching heat as an example to others. This process could take more than three days. But black market racketeering continued unabated as Margot recalled:

The black market was used mainly to obtain food and tobacco. The Dutch had a few books but they were in the Dutch language. Paper in books was used to roll tobacco to make cigarettes, even pages of the Bible. Some people had been taken off ships carrying perhaps two suitcases. Some of the Dutch had a lot of jewellery to sell. Whereas a lot of us were just fished out of the water and we only had what we stood up in. Nothing! People gave us one or two things … We didn't have shoes, we had these wooden things but they just broke so we were without shoes and had very few clothes … We cut trees down and cut them up so that we could have a fire. Otherwise we didn't have a fire. Some people had a mosquito net, but they had brought it with them. Mosquitoes were troublesome to say the least. In one camp we used to go down and get water from a tap. We boiled it, and we also boiled any water from the river if it was for drinking or cooking purposes. If it was for washing then we just used it as it was.[8]

Eventually, all women prisoners discovered ingenious ways not only to obtain food but also to make it last longer. They tried to cook rice in a variety of ways in an attempt to alter its taste and texture. They found that bread could be made by mixing rice flour and coconut milk, and if they deliberately burned rice and added boiling water, with a little imagination the resulting brew could taste like coffee. Slowly and steadily the women adapted to their changed circumstances. Moreover, their quietly courageous spirits confronted each dietary hardship and adversity in the only way possible: by creating a powerful and unique bond with one another.

Notes

1. Imperial War Museum Oral History Interview with Dame Margot Turner, ref. 9196.
2. Ibid.
3. Ibid.
4. Ibid. Incident also recorded in J. Smyth, *The Will to Live* (1970), p. 92.
5. IWM Oral History Interview with Dame Margot Turner, ref. 9196.
6. Ibid.
7. 'The War Diary of Brenda Macduff', published in the *Middlesex Hospital Nurses Benevolent Fund Journal*, December 1995, no 65, pp. 29–31.
8. IWM Oral History Interview with Dame Margot Turner, ref. 9196.

7

A Higher Authority

Within the first few weeks of their arrival at Palembang camp the women prisoners had organised an efficient system of administration. They had elected their own representatives and appointed certain leaders to be responsible for aspects of camp life. For instance, there was a leader for educational matters, for health promotion, for food distribution, for fuel gathering, for social activities and for spiritual morale. In terms of governing a community it could be argued that the women rapidly established a fair, democratic and efficient society within the confines of their compound. The class distinctions that had separated all nationalities and sectors of society before the war were totally abandoned in favour of a framework that was based on individual skills. The women had quickly realised that in order to survive they had to be organised and resourceful.

Given their dire situation it was clearly nonsense to construct a hierarchy that was based entirely on social prestige. Undoubtedly a hierarchy of sorts developed, but it was based on what people were capable of and what they could offer, although social class played some part since women in the higher social class brackets were more educated than others who had not been given the same educational opportunities. Furthermore, those women who rose instantly to the top of the hierarchy were doctors or nurses. Clearly in a place where disease was rife and hygiene paramount, this medical-based leadership was hardly surprising. These women also possessed crucial organisational skills and a wide experience of human nature, as Margot explained:

> Nurses should be self-disciplined and I think this was probably a great help to us. There were a lot of nurses in the camp and our training was a good thing. We probably looked at things in a different light to some people, and of course we were able to help people. Not that we had much to nurse with, we only had a few medicines. We also had some good doctors in the camp. We were looking after people, feeding them, washing them, you know; when people are feeling sick you have to try and make them comfortable whatever the circumstances, but that was on top of all the other work we had to do as well in the camp. We used to have a rota and take it in turns to be on duty. We selected representatives informally. Dr McDowell was the first one and someone to do with the YWCA, though complaining to the Japanese commandant very rarely yielded results. We were a very mixed bunch, British, Australian, Dutch and Indonesian ... You only knew your friends who were near you. In the first camp there was a Japanese doctor who was very kind, but he was too kind to us so he was moved. Someone else came who couldn't care less. He would say that people were fit to work when they were not – you know things like that. Some of the Japanese guards were human and they would occasionally talk about their families.[1]

Next to the medical profession in the skills hierarchy were the missionaries and teachers, primarily because of their education and the fact that they were used to dealing with large numbers of people and children, and assumed a natural air of authority. While the doctors and nurses established a camp hospital from scratch, the teachers and missionaries took charge of educational and spiritual matters. A number of school classes were set up and rudimentary lessons in mathematics, English language, geography, history and art were taught to children under the age of 12. When boys reached the age of 12 they were automatically transferred to the men's camp. Girls of 12 simply left the classroom and assisted the other women with their daily work routines. Some women had grown up with fathers, brothers or uncles who were plumbers, electricians and engineers and had managed to absorb some of their knowledge; these too were highly valued within the hierarchy of survival skills.

Gradually, out of an atmosphere of total chaos, confusion and utter despair, the women constructed a sustainable and emotionally supportive community. But one of the primary ways of dealing with Japanese superiority was to focus on the worshipping of a higher authority. Many of the nurses and teachers were nuns and, therefore, their skills and the practice of worshipping a superior being were already inextricably linked. However, as Margot recalled with some emotion, one magnificent woman stood out from all the rest for her sheer capacity to instil the will to live in others and to encourage them to look towards the future. Her name was Miss Margaret Dryburgh. Speaking of this amazing woman, Margot fondly remembered that:

We had a wonderful missionary who used to write musical notes from memory. She would write whole music concerts and was quite simply amazing. Everyone used to hum the tunes. When the concerts were held, they used to hum all these tunes; and you could sit with your eyes shut and imagine you were at a prom concert or something like that, it was wonderful.[2]

Margaret Dryburgh was a highly intelligent and discerning woman who had an unshakeable belief in God and an innate gift for making the best of any situation. Her uplifting presence permeated the camp at many levels. Margaret was born in Sunderland, of Presbyterian parents and had previously worked as a missionary in Shantou, China, before taking up a position in Singapore. Like all the others, she had been captured by the advancing Japanese forces when Singapore fell in 1942. But Margaret was an invincible character. She believed that God had given her this destiny and it was her duty to uplift her fellow prisoners. She subsequently formed a normal choir alongside a truly remarkable choir of orchestral voices, with prisoners taking the parts of violins, cellos, violas and the double bass. Another prisoner, named Norah Chambers, was a graduate of the London

Royal Academy of Music and assisted her with her work. The classical music was annotated from memory and arranged in four parts so that the women could hum the various parts of the orchestra.

Classical music compositions by Beethoven, Chopin, Handel, Mozart and Brahms echoed across the camp courtesy of the Palembang Women's Prisoner-of-War Choir. Margaret and Norah also composed some music of their own for the women to sing. To some extent this enterprise enabled the women to forget their circumstances for a while and to draw on a higher authority. Although Margaret exuded Christian charity and beliefs, she did not forcibly attempt to convert anyone to her faith. She believed instead that each person found their own way to God and chose to lead by example, since this was all that her God required of her. But in a place where such daily misery prevailed, the orchestral choir concerts were nothing less than astonishing, and for the duration of one evening a week, they provided testimony to the ability of human spirits to soar above adversity.

Margaret wrote her own musical compositions along with a diary, books and poetry. In many respects she looked upon her internment as simply another, though perhaps most unusual, opportunity to spread the word of God. For Margaret, the orchestral choir and religious worship were glorious manifestations of her innate belief in the Almighty, but on another level they were acts of defiance in the face of Japanese hostility. Margot, Netta and many others viewed the concerts as providing a constant reminder to their persecutors that a greater force existed – a being that was truly divine, rather than a Japanese emperor who merely thought he was. Margaret organised a camp magazine, held church services every Sunday in hut number nine, wrote and conducted weekly Saturday night music concerts and wrote a special captives' hymn that was sung for the first time on 5 July 1942:

> Father in Captivity
> We would lift our hearts to Thee
> Keep us ever in Thy Love
> Grant that daily we may prove
> Those who place their trust in Thee
> More than conquerors may be.

Give us patience to endure
Keep our hearts serene and pure
Grant us courage, charity
Greater faith, humility
Readiness to own Thy Will
Be we free or Captive Still.

For our country we would pray
In this hour be Thou her stay.
Pride and selfishness forgive,
Teach her by Thy laws to live
By Thy Grace may all men see
That true greatness comes from Thee.

For our loved ones we would pray
Be their guardians night and day
From all dangers keep them free
Banish all anxiety
May they trust us to Thy care
Know that Thou our pains doth share.

May the day of freedom dawn
Peace and justice be reborn
Grant that nations loving Thee
O'er the world by brothers be
Cleansed by suffering know rebirth
See Thy Kingdom come on earth.[3]

Margaret was renowned throughout the camp for her poetry, songs and, most of all, for her sound advice. When depression descended and threatened to overwhelm the women she would enthusiastically and repeatedly tell them to look upwards towards the magnificent Asian sky. This was excellent advice, for it was entirely possible to forget the confines of the prison compound when staring at the immense beauty of the tropical sky. Indeed, Margot remembered vividly the clarity of it, especially at night. Blackout conditions prevented the usual light pollution and the stars were radiant in their clearly marked constellations. Margaret never ceased to point out to all the women, including Margot, that there was no barbed wire in the sky. Thus, the order to 'look up' became a daily recommendation to all of those in despair. Nevertheless, it was impossible to get through each and every day in such adverse conditions without occasionally feeling despondent. Margot was luckier than most, in that she had a naturally optimistic outlook and a quirky, dry sense of humour, but even she had moments when everything seemed too difficult to bear. Most of these seemed to revolve around the ongoing lack of privacy. It was virtually impossible to obtain any time alone, and this problem in turn made it difficult for individual women to quietly reflect on their own thoughts and feelings. Margot noted that all women seemed to go through a process of needing some solitude:

> I think sometimes it all became too much. One used to go and sit in the middle of the compound. I got fed up of people being around me. It was not exactly boredom because you had too much to do to get bored. I think one wondered what was happening and what was going to happen next, but we always had something to do.[4]

The constant presence and chatter of other people in the prison huts and working parties did affect a lot of the women. Not having enough time or space to collect their thoughts was a problem for most. However, some convincingly argued that it was important to keep busy and occupied all the time, since too much thinking could lead to depression. As far as work was concerned, Margot recalled that nearly all the women pulled their weight. Those who were work-shy were usually chivvied into action:

> You always have a few lame ducks about the place wherever you are and whatever you are doing. But on the whole, everybody mucked in and got on with things in the circumstances. On the whole we got on. There was the odd little squabble sometimes, but you can't have six hundred women together without the odd squabble.[5]

Margaret Dryburgh and others did their best to maintain camp morale. As strange as it may have seemed, it was not unusual for the Japanese peasant guards to attend the music concerts. As the melodic voices filled the compound each Saturday evening, the guards were drawn into the concert hut more by curiosity than by invitation. They frequently expressed amazement at such beautifully constructed music and even applauded ironically and loudly at the end of British nationalistic tunes such as *Land of Hope and Glory*. One of the guards, claiming to be a Christian fellow who did not believe in war, became a regular attendee, to the point where he knew the words and even joined in some of the songs. Social activities were crucial for maintaining prisoner morale, and in addition to the classical music concerts, prisoners staged mock fashion shows, poetry recitals and comedy evenings, where the Japanese guards were mimicked and became the butt of all jokes. General knowledge quizzes were held and there were also attempts to make traditional games. Margot was intrigued by this latter process:

> Someone made cards out of a set of photographs so they could play bridge. A Chinese girl got bits of wood and made a marjong for us, which if we had some spare time we would play. But latterly it was all work and you didn't have the strength to play.[6]

Despite the deplorable conditions of camp life, the efforts of missionaries and nuns did have an extremely positive effect on the women's morale and spiritual well-being overall. In addition, by reminding them of a higher divine authority, the power of Japanese guards was symbolically and spiritually diminished. Religious observance was also a way of keeping track of time. Church services and strict adherence to religious festivals provided a sense of yearly rhythm. Thus the soft tones of weary prisoners and their children singing *Silent Night* could be heard reverberating around the camp every Christmas Eve, and a resounding rendition of *Thine be the Glory* heralded the dawn of Easter. One Christmas Day the Japanese guards allowed a visit from a Roman Catholic priest. Women made Christmas presents, cards and fake plum puddings. They also staged nativity plays and parties for the children.

Throughout the year they made gifts and acknowledged each other's birthdays and special occasions.

But with no news of the outside world it was difficult for some women to focus on the future. Japanese guards were usually clipped and expressionless when issuing their orders, and with no news of their men folk many women began to turn their faces to the wall in alarming numbers. These women usually died during the night, just before dawn. Those who witnessed their demise were often haunted by the strange tune of a tropical jungle bird that seemed to sing at their passing. The bird was eventually nicknamed the 'death bird' and all manner of ghostly stories and myths were invented around this jungle creature. Margot was a no-nonsense, matter-of-fact personality, however, and none of this fanciful story telling permeated her sound common-sense approach to life. Speaking of her beliefs and those of her close friend Netta Smith, Margot stated:

> We just had faith in our country, which was just as well. I think this is where some people couldn't see into the future and just gave up. You have got to have the will to live. Certainly you have got to have a sense of humour or you would never have survived. You needed to see the funny side of things even though it was pretty black. We knew we would win the war, and that thought was very firmly in our minds. We never discussed it with them [the Japanese guards], never discussed it at all, but we had no doubt. We just hoped we could hang on. It became more difficult when the Japanese military took over. Sometimes we used to get senior Japanese officers visiting the camp but nobody from the Red Cross or anything like that. When the Japanese officers came we were all told to clean the camp ready for inspection. Lots of things happened that you simply did not see and you just had to guess at what was happening. I always knew that we would win the war, I never had any doubt at all, but each year it became more difficult. We were all in the same circumstances.[7]

Margot and her companions had no idea of how the war was progressing, but it was possible to detect a change in the attitudes of their Japanese guards, and when the peasant guards were replaced by a more sinister and stricter security regime administered by the Kempeitai, it was obvious to all

Lieutenant-General Percival leaving plane on his arrival in Singapore as the new GOC Malaya. Courtesy of Imperial War Museum collection No 700-10

2. Lieutenant-General Percival, GOC Malaya (second from right), with war correspondents in Singapore, shortly before the capitulation, late January 1942.

Lieutenant-General Percival and his party carry the Union Jack on their way to surrender Singapore the Japanese. Courtesy of Imperial War Museum collection No 5707-03

4. Attack on Pearl Harbor, 7 December 1941. Photograph taken from a Japanese plane during the torpedo attack on ships moored on both sides of Ford Island. Courtesy of NHHC Collection

5. Scene on board USS *Yorktown* shortly after she was hit by three Japanese bombs on 4 June 1942. Courtesy of US National Archives Collection

. USS *Arizona* burning at Pearl Harbor, 7 December 1941. Courtesy of US National Archives
Collection

. Battle of Midway, June 1942. USS *Yorktown* (CV-5) is hit on the port side, amidships, by planes from
the carrier *Hiryu*. Courtesy of US National Archives Collection

8. The sinking of Japanese cruiser *Mikuma*, 6 June 1942. Courtesy of US National Archives Collection

9. A section of a map displaying the locations of Japanese prisoner-of-war camps for Allied personnel during the Second World War. Courtesy of Medical Research Committee of American Ex-Prisoners of War, Inc. Research and proof of authenticity by France Worthington Lipe

Some delivered prisoners of war from a Japanese internment camp Palembang on Sumatra. Courtesy of Tropenmuseum of the Royal Tropical Institute (KIT)

English prisoners of war wait on a platform Palembang. Courtesy of Tropenmuseum of the Royal Tropical Institute (KIT)

12. Aftermath of the
Hiroshima bomb.
Courtesy of www.chinfo
navy.mil/chinfoprivacy.
html

13. Atomic bombing of
Nagasaki on 9 August
1945. This picture was
taken from one of the
B-29 Superfortresses used
in the attack. Courtesy
of www.archives.
gov/research_room/
research_topics/world_
war_2_photos/images/
ww2_1623.jpg

14. Portrait photograph taken of General MacArthur in 1943 or 1944. The original print is inscribed: 'To Admiral Nimitz. With regard and admiration. Douglas MacArthur.'

15. General MacArthur, Franklin D. Roosevelt and Admiral Nimitz in Pearl Harbor, 26 July 1944. Courtesy of US Archive ARCWEB

16. Surrender of the Japanese aboard USS *Missouri*. Admiral Chester Nimitz signs the instrument of surrender.

17. Allied prisoners of war at Aomori camp near Yokohama cheer rescuers from the US Navy. Courtesy of Defense Imagery

18. Studio portrait of Staff Nurse Vivian Bullwinkel, Australian Army Nursing Service (AANS), in service dress uniform. Courtesy of Australian War Memorial

in the camp that things were not going well for the Japanese. Food shortages also indicated that perhaps a naval blockade was preventing imports. In fact, there had been several significant battles between the Allies and the Japanese since the fall of Singapore, of which the prisoners of Palembang were understandably unaware.

The first decisive victory for the Allies came about during the naval battle of Midway, which took place between 3 and 6 June 1942. Under the command of Yamamoto, a strategic plan was executed that involved dividing the combined fleet into eight task forces designed to stage a series of attacks on the atoll of the Midway. The Japanese aim was to coax Admiral Nimitz's fleet away from Pearl Harbor and force a confrontation at sea. However, Admiral Nimitz had prior knowledge of these Japanese plans courtesy of the American intelligence service. Armed with this crucial knowledge he was able to muster two task forces, under the command of Rear Admiral Fletcher, which were able to meet up at the northern point of the island and await the Japanese attack. The result was a decisive victory for the Allies, as the *Daily Express* war correspondent C. Thompson reported:

THOUSANDS OF INVADERS DIED IN THE MIDWAY BATTLE

More than 15 Jap ships – half the main force – were 'casualties' in the Battle of Midway, and thousands of Japanese perished, it is disclosed tonight in a communiqué issued in Pearl Harbour by Admiral Chester Nimitz. The Japanese were closely clustered when the American bombers swept down on it, and the Japs were so hard pressed that they did not stop to pick up survivors.

Admiral Nimitz's report, which is incomplete, covers the first three days of action. There may be more news of damage to the enemy yet to come. Naval experts believe that some of the Jap ships attacked must have lost every man on board. Admiral Nimitz's report and other news from the Pacific caused an air of suppressed elation among Washington higher-ups today. Realists who earlier showed only cautious optimism wore the look of good news on their faces. The cheerful spirit infected today's meeting of the Pacific War Council. New Zealand's Minister, Walter Nash, said as he left: 'The President's report was full of good news – good news right through.'[8]

The remarkable American victory at Midway set the stage for the first American offensive, which was staged at Guadalcanal. The Japanese had lost four fleet carriers and many experienced pilots at Midway and their defeat was keenly felt. More importantly for the Allies, the Japanese had lost their strategic advantage. The inhabitants of Palembang, however, were totally unaware of the remarkable Allied success. Some, like Margot, Netta, Dr McDowell and Margaret, were living on their faith, while others were turning their faces to the wall. The resourceful women of Palembang camp were fighting their own strategic battles, against despondency, tyranny, malnutrition, degradation and disease.

Notes

1. Imperial War Museum Oral History Interview with Dame Margot Turner, ref. 9196.
2. Ibid.
3. L. Warner & J. Sandilands, *Women Beyond the Wire* (1982), p. 137. The Captives' Hymn was sung by prisoners every week for the entirety of their internment, even when the Kempeitai took over the administration of camps and prevented concerts. Margaret Dryburgh was eventually the subject of a film entitled *Paradise Road*, with actress Pauline Collins playing the title role.
4. IWM Oral History Interview with Dame Margot Turner, ref. 9196.
5. Ibid.
6. Ibid.
7. Ibid.
8. *Daily Express* front-page story, 11 June 1942.

8

Confronting Diseases

During the three and a half years that Margot was interned at the hands of the Japanese, just over a third of all women in the camps died. In the men's camp this figure was even higher since they lost over half their number. This discrepancy between survival figures was largely due to the fact that many more of the men were already severely wounded when they were captured, and that their camps tended to be based in swamp areas where the incidence of malaria, including cerebral malaria, was much higher. The women's camp contained more medical personnel and, in terms of sanitation and hygiene, they appeared to be more organised. All doctors and nurses were acutely aware of the importance of basic hygiene, and of isolating those prisoners who displayed the symptoms of infectious diseases. They practised strict barrier nursing when appropriate, boiled clean rags for bandages and allowed them to bake in the scorching sun to destroy bacteria, and provided comfort and encouragement as best they could. They also built an effective sick bay and later a hospital, as the numbers of sick increased, and always ensured that extra rations were apportioned to those who were most in need.

Medical instruments and medicines were in extremely short supply because the contents of Red Cross food and medical parcels, intended for the prisoners, were usually commandeered by Japanese guards. Rudimentary stethoscopes were therefore constructed from bamboo, and hospital mattresses were sewn together from sacking and dried plant leaves. Some of the native women also formulated drugs from plant juice. The nurses in particular were extremely resourceful and they needed to be, since the Japanese continually hoarded medicines that were stolen from Red Cross parcels in case they were needed for their own troops. Margot stressed that to begin with:

> Doctors had some drugs but these had to be used sparingly, and we were always short of quinine for malaria patients. When the war was over they found 'go down' stores full of food and medicine. They hadn't let us have any of it, which was a terrible thing really because it might have saved a few more lives.[1]

Whilst the women were interned in Palembang, the Charitas Hospital became a central feature in their battles against disease. The hospital buildings were situated in a lush green valley and separated into three distinct areas. One area was designated for civilian women, another for civilian men and the third for military personnel. Japanese guards paraded sternly up and down the interlinking corridors to ensure the separation of these areas and kept a watchful eye on the nuns' activities. In the centre of the complex lay a lovingly tended and well-sheltered garden. This oasis of serenity was used by the nuns for prayer and meditation.

The hospital had been established by Dutch Roman Catholic nuns, and the order was headed by Sister Catherine, who had successfully managed to hide some medicines and food deep within the walls and cellars of the hospital long before the Japanese arrival. Throughout 1942 and the early part of 1943 these items were smuggled out of the hospital confines to all those who were in urgent need in the camps. Margot, who had been tenderly nursed back to health by the Charitas nuns following her shipwreck experience, had repaid the favour by working long hours at the hospital as a theatre sister, until she was thrown unceremoniously into Palembang prison for six months. It was not until long after the war that Margot realised that she had been imprisoned largely because she was suspected of being a spy.

Unbeknown to Margot, the Charitas nuns were not quite as innocent as they may have first appeared. They had constructed a clandestine spy network that had grown rapidly since the Japanese occupation and they had formulated their own forms of resistance to the enemy. In addition to smuggling medicines beneath their voluminous habits, they carried numerous messages between the hospital, its patients and the internment camps. They also ran an efficient money exchange system. Furthermore, one of the Dutch surgeons in the hospital had managed to conceal a radio in his accommodation quarters and regular broadcast bulletins were passed between the surgeon, the bishop of Palembang, the hospital superintendent and the nuns and patients of Charitas Hospital. Parcels, letters and coded messages were secreted out of the hospital and into the city and the internment camps. Prisoners even managed to exchange food and birthday gifts during this stage of their captivity. Midwives were particularly useful in this respect, since their work naturally required them to leave the hospital and make home visits on numerous occasions.

This trafficking of information conspired to temporarily reunite wives and husbands. These clandestine meetings often took place in the rather unromantic patients' toilets, since these were usually unguarded. Each prisoner-of-war camp had a leader who was responsible for representing the needs of the prisoners to the Japanese officials, though representation did not always have the desired effect. Leaders also took it upon themselves to try and better the lot of their fellow prisoners. The British leader in Margot's camp, Dr Jean McDowell, was a Scottish lady with a soft Highland voice and tolerant manner. Alongside her normal, everyday work she regularly invented a wide variety of symptoms and excuses for her female patients that would necessitate a visit to the Charitas Hospital. These feigned visits would coincide with that of their husbands.

The hospital superintendent, Mother Alacoque, who looked as though she was a picture of demure innocence, was actually the mastermind behind all the plots and clandestine activity. Women secreted messages in their corsets, and some decided that the only safe place for hiding information was within the intimate linings of their sanitary towels. But the web of conspiracy was gradually infiltrated by the Japanese secret police, the Kempeitai. They eventually caught one woman carrying a large number of messages on her person, and after a brutal series of interrogations and investigations, the Charitas Hospital was closed down in September 1943. The unfortunate female courier was never seen again.

Fearing that her activities might actually be discovered, Mother Alacoque had already taken the precaution of hiding stocks of her precious medicines in a variety of safe houses, but some of these were discovered by the Kempeitai and the remaining supply did not last long. The medicines were not replenished and the demise of Charitas Hospital signalled an end to effective communication between the male and female internment camps. Margot noted that as soon as the hospital was closed the prisoners were told to build a hospital within the camp compound, and the nuns became prisoners alongside Margot:

> The guards viewed us as coolies I suppose. The nuns that were nurses were there permanently and we used to help them. I suppose we used to help them half the time and do the camp chores the other half of the time. But it depended on which camp we were in and how many sick patients there were. We were able to help some people, but for others we just made them comfortable. We could sometimes get hold of the odd aspirin but we had very little to nurse with. We were feeding them, washing them and making them comfortable, but that was on top of everything else we had to do.[2]

In the absence of pharmaceutical drugs, medical personnel had to derive their own home cures for some of the most common ailments. To combat dysentery, for instance, patients were instructed to drink cold tea, and when this was no longer available they were encouraged to eat ground charcoal. Rock sulphur was found to alleviate some skin conditions and charcoal mixed with the ashes of firewood alleviated griping stomach pains. In addition to dysentery, the most common medical conditions were malaria, cholera, tuberculosis, scabies and beriberi. The latter was caused by vitamin B deficiency and took two distinct forms: sufferers either produced so much toxic tissue fluid that they literally drowned as their bodies began to swell and their lungs were filled with an overload of pleural fluid; or they shrivelled away to skin and bone as their bodies succumbed to the atrophic version of the condition.

There were also a few cases of poliomyelitis, tuberculosis and some more obscure fevers that were never identified. The doctors and nurses referred to them simply as 'Banka fever' because they had no way of testing blood to identify them. Margot believed that the fever was some form of cerebral malaria. The anopheline mosquitoes were responsible for the spread of malaria and only a few people had mosquito nets. Attempts to keep mosquitoes out of the prison huts were futile and bites often became sore and infected. Some people appeared to have a natural immunity to malaria and cigarette smokers tended not be bitten to quite the same degree as non-smokers. However, Margot maintained that a lot of women, herself included, tried to get hold of tobacco not to prevent mosquito bites, but because a cigarette staved off hunger pangs:

> I don't smoke any more, but then, at that time, it was very useful to smoke because if you had a cigarette you didn't feel so hungry you see. Cigarettes were very helpful in that respect. Tobacco must have that effect, you know, it must stop hunger in some way.[3]

Taking care of sick prisoners was a full-time job, but nurses were initially required to carry out laborious and heavy routine chores around the camp in addition to their professional work. Sick bays tended to be stifling and foul smelling, regardless of how often the drains and latrines were scoured. During the monsoon season the foul effluent from inadequate drains rose up in torrents and flooded the entire camp. In addition to this deluge of sewage, the Japanese guards were apt to answer their calls of nature whenever and wherever they pleased, often in full view of the women. Heat and humidity provided a wonderful breeding ground for rats, fleas and infection, though on the plus side maggots did an amazing job in terms of cleaning wounds and sores since they fed on the dead flesh and prevented septicaemia. Mosquito bites, however, often became septic because of malnutrition, and a lack of clean water prompted several outbreaks of urinary tract disease. A skin condition that caused extreme itching was prevalent in all the camps and was most likely due to a vitamin deficiency. On a practical day-to-day level, tropical storms also hindered medical care, as one nurse recorded in her diary:

We had a most unpleasant experience last night. There was a very bad storm on – lightning, thunder and heavy rain. I was on duty in a dysentery ward. One of the two rotten little Japanese oil lamps had blown out and it was very dark. Then suddenly there was a terrific clap of thunder and I saw sparks flying around. Then the screaming began. I ran out of the ward and saw the 'attap' of the roof of the bathroom a few yards away on fire. It was put out within ten minutes, but whilst it lasted it was pretty frightening. I got all the patients up in case it spread. The fire and sparks were caused, they say, by a fireball. One of the Indonesian policemen on guard and holding a rifle at the time, collapsed and he died the following day.[4]

Nursing in the grim bleakness of the prison hut hospitals was very basic and there was little the nurses could do to save many of their patients. It was simply a case of providing comfort to them in their last days. They listened to their worries, sponged them with cool water when they were feverish and gave them additional warmth with extra blankets when they were shivering from the effects of malaria. They would turn their immobilised patients to prevent the development of pressure sores and coax their circulation by massaging their muscles and spine. As the war progressed malnutrition levels increased and even those with a previously strong constitution succumbed to illness, including the medical staff. Margot suffered a bout of Banka fever but recovered after a few days:

> I had a fever, a very high temperature and I stayed on my boards for a day or so. I had it once or twice in the early days after I came home but not since, so I don't think it was malaria, I think it was Banka fever. It was the survival of the fittest of course, and those who were the fittest had to do most of the work, like digging the graves and burying the dead. People were just so weak you see, they couldn't do things because they had no strength. They could not see a future, especially if their husbands had died. This is what happened you see, because the Japanese would not tell them that their husbands had died to begin with, they would tell them six months later. Or they would tell the men that their wives had died, it was terrible really, but they never told them straight away.[5]

Most women who suffered from Banka fever did not recover. The disease was characterised by high temperatures, lapses into unconsciousness and bright red skin rashes. Dengue fever was also a problem. The women began to kiss each other goodnight every evening before bed just in case they did not live to see the next day. Indeed, the number of deaths reached epidemic proportions and the Japanese eventually decided to relieve nurses of their extra camp duties because they were needed to work longer hours in the hospital. Women realised for the first time, and with a growing level of despondency, that they were more likely to die of malaria or Banka fever than they were to survive their ordeal. Women stood guard over the bodies of those who had died in the night, which were left in an open-ended, makeshift wooden shed called a 'pendapo' in the middle of the camp compound. They buried them at first light.

> The dying began in earnest in the last month of 1944. In late November there were 210 victims of Banka fever lying in the huts and, as December began, there were six deaths, all Englishwomen and hence almost certainly of slender means. Three nuns died in as many weeks and on Christmas Eve the tally stood at fifteen. Christmas, which had stood out so bravely as a landmark for the past two years, could not stand up to this assault and served only to underline the descent into sickness and the beginnings of despair. Miss Dryburgh held a short quiet service on Christmas Day. 'We couldn't even sing', said Phyllis Briggs [captured British nurse]. 'Most of us had lost our voices but anyway there was an apathy that had never existed before.'[6]

The camp death rate continued to accelerate in the first few months of 1945 and seventy-seven women lost their lives in January alone.[7]

Funerals averaged at about four a day in the coming months and the will to live became a paramount survival tool. Margot adopted a pragmatic approach:

> The thing was you had to keep going – I mean, you could have a high temperature one day and have to lie down on your mat and if you didn't get up the next day you would probably never get up again. I feel very strongly that quite a lot of people who died shouldn't have done so but they just gave

up. I know that I wanted to live. I wanted to get home and see my family. But there were people who could see no reason for continuing, and that was very sad.[8]

Faced with the alarming proposition that they too might succumb to the epidemic, Japanese guards were eventually told to inoculate the prisoners against cholera and typhoid in the hope that Banka fever might have some connection to these diseases. Nurses set up an outreach nursing service similar to district nurses in an attempt to keep the sick patients from infecting each other, and doctors continued to plead for quinine and other medicines, such as morphia, to at least relieve the pain of those who were dying.

But the death toll continued to rise and there was no pain relief forthcoming. In some camps doctors were forced by the Japanese guards to falsify death certificates so that malnutrition was not recorded as a direct cause of death. To make matters worse, by this point the Indonesian peasant guards and the civilian Japanese guards had been replaced by the dreaded Kempeitai.

Notes

1. Imperial War Museum Oral History Interview with Dame Margot Turner, ref. 9196.
2. Ibid.
3. Ibid.
4. 'The War Diary of Brenda Macduff', published in the *Middlesex Hospital Nurses Benevolent Fund Journal*, December 1995, no 65, pp. 29–31.
5. IWM Oral History Interview with Dame Margot Turner, ref. 9196.
6. L. Warner & J. Sandilands, *Women Beyond the Wire* (1982), p. 221.
7. Ibid., p. 222.
8. IWM Oral History Interview with Dame Margot Turner, ref. 9196.

9

The Kempeitai

U p until 1 April 1944 the administration of Margot's internment camp lay in the hands of peasant Japanese and Indonesian guards. As Margot and others had quickly noted, these guards were not particularly intelligent and it was relatively easy for prisoners to tease and ridicule them. Members of the Imperial Japanese Army did likewise, and referred to these men as their inferiors and called them Hei Hoes. On the plus side, however, the prisoners could sometimes forge a reasonable relationship with the Hei Hoes and a few women of dubious character even offered them sexual favours in return for black market goods. Although the interminable and often impromptu Tenkos were a distasteful humiliation for all prisoners, as long as the women bowed very low during the roll calls and each time they set eyes on a guard, they were generally left to their own devices to get on with their assigned work. But in April 1944 Japanese military secret police, otherwise known as the Kempeitai, assumed control of the camp, headed by a new commandant named Captain Siki.

The Kempeitai were the Japanese equivalent to the German Gestapo, and shared many of their methods in terms of interrogation and torture techniques. They swore allegiance to Emperor Hirohito, who was supposedly viewed by all Japanese as being part-god and part-man, and they claimed to follow the ancient way of the samurai. In addition to maintaining military discipline, and arresting dissenters and spies, they provided information, encouragement and practical support to the F-Kikan intelligence group. This latter group was largely responsible for persuading disaffected British Indian soldiers to fight on the side of the Japanese, in return making vague promises to support their moves towards an independent India at the end of the war. The tentacles of the Kempeitai stretched across numerous military and industrial networks. Furthermore, all members of the Japanese Imperial Guard were equally fanatical about serving their country, and children as young as 6 were dressed in military uniform and indoctrinated into the ways of the warrior. The following extract is taken from a letter to the parents of a new military recruit from his commanding officer:

> We have learned that your son will shortly experience the greatest joy and satisfaction possible to one of our nation by joining soon our company. We congratulate you. When your son enters the barracks, the officers of the company will take your place in looking after his welfare. We will be to him as a stern father and a loving mother. We will always be concerned with his two-fold training, body and mind, so that in belonging to the Army he may become a good soldier and a loyal subject of the Emperor. We want to be able to teach him in such a way that he may realise the highest hope of a member of our race, that is, to die for the Emperor.[1]

As a mission statement, this was hardly likely to appeal to most Western parents, but for the Japanese, acceptance into the army was considered to be a great honour. Training was extremely brutal and recruits were beaten on a daily basis. They were taught to eat without chewing, since each meal had to be finished within a period of three minutes; toilet visits were timed in a regimented fashion; and uniform and equipment checks were elaborate and needlessly fastidious in nature. Every aspect of a soldier's life was moulded to worship his country and his emperor. Minor misdemeanours produced shared mass punishments, and a stoical army emerged that was reared on mythological stories of ancient Japanese warriors and military glories. Moreover, these myths were taught as though they were genuine historical facts. Thus military recruits appeared to believe that their emperor was indeed a demigod and a direct descendant of the mythical sun goddess Amaterasu, who according to legend had created the Japanese islands.

As part of their training Kempeitai officers were taught sadistic but usually effective torture techniques. These included water punishments, whereby victims were bound and water was poured through their nose and mouth until they lost consciousness, and searing hot irons and other metal tools were used to inflict severe pain on ear drums, sex organs and other sensitive body areas. There was also a complex system of wooden poles and ropes which bound victims up in a specific way in order for Kempeitai officers to jump on various body parts – a process which would agonisingly rip joints from their sockets. Other torture methods were similar to those used by the Gestapo, such as ripping toe and fingernails from their nail beds and flogging victims on floors of broken glass. The chief objective was to extract information from victims and inflict as much pain and suffering as possible while doing so. The Kempeitai had a reputation that surpassed all others in terms of punishment and retribution, and they considered themselves to be the elite military police force of the Japanese Imperial Army.

Not surprisingly, given their notions of an all-conquering Japanese empire and samurai legend and discipline, the prospect of running female prisoner-of-war camps did not fit comfortably with Kempeitai officers. For them, a front-line combatant position was infinitely preferable to being the jailors of a bunch of bedraggled, malnourished and alien women. They subsequently ruled them with malicious intent. Hinting at future brutal punishments, threatening extreme torture and unleashing all forms of psychological warfare, Kempeitai officers exerted an entirely new regime of prison camp government. Denied the honour of having a proper soldier's role, they vented their sheer frustration, humiliation and anger on their already browbeaten and weary female charges. As Margot vividly recalled, this transference from civilian to military supervision marked a dramatic sea change in their treatment:

Food rations were halved as soon as the Kempeitai assumed control. We were allowed half a cup of tea per person per month, and one kerosene tin of red palm oil was issued – not much for six hundred people. Tenkos became more frequent and labour intensified. The choir was immediately banned, along with concerts and religious services of any nature. They put a stop to all that. The greatest hardship was the lack of soap, and when there was no water the only way to wash was to stand out in the rain. They would also tell the women when their husbands had died, but again, not straight away. It was difficult you see, because you could not always believe what they were saying. Sometimes they told the truth and other times they were just saying things for the sake of it.[2]

Kempeitai officers adopted a very different and sadistic approach to the women. They humiliated them at every opportunity and Tenkos became more violent in nature. The ever-tolerant Dr Jean McDowell, for instance, was viciously slapped on numerous occasions for allowing too many prisoners to languish in their hospital beds instead of attending roll calls and completing arduous workloads. Officers also took to watching and leering at the women as they bathed at the communal tong:

> It was a bit alarming to begin with, but it didn't worry me unduly. When I went to the wash room to have my daily dipper bath, a Japanese guard just stood and looked at me, just to see what a white woman looked like in the nude. But it was much better not to worry about them and to feel cool with a wash. Our diet was so poor that after a few months we stopped menstruating. Everybody stopped having periods, which was a good thing really because nothing was ever supplied for us in that way, so really it was a mercy. People couldn't do things, they had no energy, no strength and most of them were ill.[3]

Whereas before some women had offered guards sexual favours in return for black market supplies, the new officers adopted an altogether different system for satisfying their sexual needs. Each night they entered the prison compound and the prison hospital searching for suitable women to rape. Some women fought back and were brutally wounded as a result. Others were sadistically tortured by guards who insisted on giving the women electric shock treatment while their bodies were wet and naked. Every night the women lived in fear of being chosen by the Kempeitai, since many did not return in the morning. Evidence suggests that the Japanese government was complicit in such conduct. A cohort of native prostitutes known as the 'comfort corps' was also provided to army officers. It is estimated that over 220,000 Japanese and Indonesian girls were forcibly recruited into the comfort corps. One girl recalled her experiences as follows:

> On arrival, the women, with feet bleeding from the long forced march, came under the supervision of the sergeant in charge of canteens, who chose the most attractive to serve the officers. As he instructed her: 'This is the same as being on the front line. You will now look after the officers and will have to work harder than before for your country.' He taught her how to bow in greeting to each officer and again thanking him after the service was completed. The sergeant himself would earn points for the quality of service given by the women under his care.[4]

For higher-ranking officers only virginal young girls would suffice:

> Nagase Takashi wandered off to visit comfort women on his days off. For a short period he was posted as a Japanese language instructor to the harbour island of Sentosa. Twelve Korean girls had been unloaded there and he remembers how the virgins were all reserved for the notorious commanding officer, Lt Miki, 'who first tasted each one by one'. He tells of the girls' sorrow in their dismal language classes, and at the end of the interview he weeps, saying in a whisper: 'I am very, very sorry for what we have done here during war time.'[5]

The Japanese government justified prostitution on the grounds that it maintained the morale of troops and reduced the risk of venereal disease. However, there was no official justification for the rape of women prisoners. Margot was eternally grateful that the good Lord had chosen to make her tall and big boned. Japanese men were much shorter than the British and Dutch generally and they preferred their womenfolk to be even shorter. Fortunately for Margot, the guards found her height and statuesque build very intimidating and she was left alone.

Undoubtedly the new military administration did increase levels of collective fear within the camp. Mental manipulation was seen as a crucial key in controlling the prisoners. Therefore, women were told of sinister punishments that would be likely meted out to them if they did not comply with orders. Emphasis was placed on undermining their confidence and making them believe that Japan was ultimately going to triumph over the Allies. Kempeitai officers also seemed to become bored more easily than their Hei Hoe counterparts. They had been trained to kill on the battlefield and, apart from taking their anger and frustration out on the women, they were prone to attacking any animals that had the misfortune to cross their daily paths. It was not unusual, therefore, for women to witness wounded cats crawling pitifully around the camps with their insides trailing on the ground; they were simply the victims of Kempeitai bayonet practice. For the children in particular this was a distressing sight. From a more practical point of view, as Margot recalled, the random process of killing cats also led to plagues of rats, since wild cats had provided the only effective weapon against the rodents.

The Kempeitai initiated behavioural changes and prisoners were increasingly regimented. Tenkos became more frequent and acts of violence against the women occurred on an almost daily basis. Captain Siki insisted on giving propaganda speeches each morning about the amazing advances that were being made by Japanese forces and old, out-of-date newspapers that told of such advances were distributed around the camp. Prisoners were gathered daily in national groups and presented one at a time for Siki's inspection. Their nationality and age details were recorded in a large, bound book. Even small babies were presented to the new commandant. All prisoners were subsequently weighed every month and camp work was organised with military precision. Margot described this new phase of rule as almost unbearable:

> The worst and most debilitating innovation was the amount of heavy manual labour we were forced to undertake. Working parties had to be organised to unload the rations, which were brought in to the camp in military lorries. The sacks of rice, which formed the greater part of the supplies, would have taxed our strength severely even if we had been in good physical condition; but in our debilitated state the work of moving sacks left us utterly exhausted.
>
> Siki then announced that, as the food situation in Sumatra was becoming acute, the prisoners would be required to cultivate gardens within the camp

for their vegetable supply. The area we had to dig was the space in the centre of the camp, consisting of hard clay, and also some ground outside the camp. All the digging had to be done with heavy hoes which made little impression on the iron-hard ground and jarred the diggers horribly at every stroke. In addition, we had to tidy up the roads outside the camp, including the gardens of the houses in which the Japs were living, and clean their drains daily.

The water supply in this camp was very poor and often we only had one tin of water in which to wash ourselves and our clothes; and the drinking water was very limited indeed. It is not difficult to imagine the hardship imposed by this lack of water; after all the filthy and dirty jobs we were forced to do we virtually never got clean. Some of the prisoners were allowed to go, in the heat of the afternoon, to fetch buckets of water from a hydrant about half a mile down the road. But first they had to fill the baths of Japanese houses, and then water the gardens in the camp, which were hard and bone dry. This water fatigue meant several trips to the hydrant, but after all their labour they would be lucky to get one bucket of drinking water into the camp.

All this heavy manual work went on – in a tropical climate – every day from 5 a.m. to 6 p.m., with a break of three hours in the middle of the day (except for those who wanted extra water and went out in the scorching sun). The British prisoners protested strongly that many of our members were quite unfit to undertake this arduous labour, but all our protests were unavailing. This, more than any other single factor, accounted for the many deaths of prisoners in the following months.[6]

Since Siki's garden initiative was first implemented in August, it was not surprising that more women died. The weather was extremely hot and very humid. Even those who managed to survive still wilted and succumbed to sunstroke as they worked in the tropical heat with little water. Siki was also apt to point out that the British prisoners protested about hard labour far more than the Dutch. In many respects this was the case, but they had, after all, been working this way for much longer, since they had been working for the Dutch from the outset to gain money for the black market. The urgent need for vegetable gardens, however, was the first clear sign to the prisoners that their captors were under pressure.

During the following days there were other indications that the all-conquering Japanese army was experiencing problems. Delivering one of his regular and extensive propaganda speeches to the prisoners one morning, Siki announced that there was a growing risk of air raids. He firmly instructed them, in stilted English, to evacuate the camp and run to a nearby rubber plantation if they heard the siren. As he stressed the imminent danger, Siki told the prisoners not to be afraid, and then quickly assured them that if they were caught up in the bombing he would bravely die with them. Siki did not for one minute, however, understand why all the women in the camp let out an almighty cheer at this announcement. Irony was clearly lost on the Kempeitai.

The Allies had launched successful air raids on Palembang, Banka and other areas of Sumatra on 11 August 1944, even though the Americans were experiencing considerable difficulties in terms of recruiting medical back-up personnel for their troops, particularly women. Unlike British women who had rushed to swell the ranks of military nurses at the outbreak of war, American women did not rally to the cause in quite the same way. The situation was so dire at one point that eleven American hospital units were sent overseas without their complement of nurses, and over a thousand US Army nurses were hospitalised, suffering from exhaustion.

The one group of women who were eager to join up, however, were Chinese Americans, such as Helen Pon Onyett, who remembered vividly the passion and excitement she felt at being able to display her American patriotism and her Chinese nationalism by joining the military. She firmly believed that:

> The armed forces might provide a space in which she could be judged by other Americans on the basis of her skills, not her race. For her, this hope was fulfilled: 'I was treated as a nurse, not an oriental somebody.'[7]

Others were not so happy about their enlistment or their experiences and it seemed that American military nursing structures were not so disciplined as their British counterparts. An American military nurse recruit named Lavonne Camp complained:

I found the perils of preserving my virtue in a testosterone-laden world were just as consuming as worrying about a Japanese submarine torpedoing our troopship. Those were the days before sexual harassment was considered an issue ... I saw splendid professional people succumb to alcohol abuse and sexual profligacy, probably not for the duration, but that behaviour, too, becomes a memory.[8]

Perhaps these problems did not beset the British military nursing sections because of their rigid discipline systems and long-standing Nightingale traditions. But whatever the reasons for American disenchantment, President Roosevelt was forced to make an emotional and patriotic appeal to Congress to amend the Selective Service Act so as to provide for the induction of military nurses because the need was too urgent to wait any longer for volunteers to the cause. The *New York Times* reported his heartfelt appeal on 7 January 1945:

It is tragic that the gallant women who have volunteered for service as nurses should be so overworked. It is tragic that our wounded men should ever want for the best possible nursing care. The inability to get the needed nurses for the Army is not due to any shortage of nurses. Two hundred and eighty thousand nurses are now practising in this country. It has been estimated by the War Manpower Commission that twenty-seven thousand additional nurses could be made available to the armed forces without interfering too seriously with the needs of the civilian population for nurses. Since volunteering has not produced the number of nurses required, I urge that the Selective Service Act be amended to provide for the induction of nurses into the armed forces. The need is too pressing to await the outcome of further efforts at recruiting. The care and treatment given to our wounded and sick soldiers has been the best known to medical science. Those standards must be maintained at all costs. We cannot tolerate a lowering of them by failure to provide adequate nursing for the brave men who stand desperately in need of it.[9]

Ironically, while the US Army was desperately struggling to entice nurse recruits into their ranks, in Britain government restrictions had already been put in place which curtailed the number of nurses entering the military, because all British trained nurses were queuing up in their thousands to join the armed forces. There was no doubt, however, that nurses were needed by all the Allied forces at this point in the war. Preparations were being made for further offensives and medical care for the wounded was vital. By now the Japanese had resorted to kamikaze attacks on American carrier forces, and these were initially successful. Over 2,000 attacks took place against the American fleet at Okinawa and more in the Philippines. Throughout April 1945 over 1,400 Japanese suicide missions were staged from Kyushu in an attempt to defend Japanese territory. During this period twenty-six Allied ships were sunk and 160 ships were severely damaged. Eventually Allied forces became more astute at avoiding kamikaze attacks and, since there were no returning Japanese pilots, the impact of such offensives in the long run were diminished.

Once the Allies had established air bases on Okinawa, American bombers were within easy striking distance of Japan and strategic bombing raids began in earnest. Fifteen square miles of Tokyo were obliterated, particularly the industrial area. In addition, industrial bases in Nagoya, Yokohama, Osaka and Kobe were destroyed. In the meantime, the Pacific fleet, with assistance from British carriers, continued to put pressure on Japanese forces.

There was no doubt that the Allies were making excellent progress despite their logistical medical and nursing problems. Furthermore, for the women who were interned deep in Japanese jungle camps, the mere sight of an Allied plane ignited their hope. Some prisoners experienced spine-tingling elation as the air raid became visible to the camp's inhabitants. On one occasion the women in Margot's camp felt the sheer joy of spotting one of the Allied planes soaring up into the sky after one of the frequent raids on Palembang. After the grim, dismal years of struggle and deprivation, Margot claimed that this first sighting of the Allies did wonders in terms of reviving their spirits:

> There was a big oil installation at Palembang and there was a heavy bombing raid just before we were moved again. We were thrilled to see Allied raids, [laughs] the Japs kept telling us to get back into our huts; they weren't so pleased to see our planes. That is why they moved us to the last camp deep in the jungle. The Allied raids increased just before we were moved to the last

camp. We hoped that the Allies realised that we were down there. I do think that's why we were moved.[10]

There were other signs that changes were afoot. On 17 August 1944 the first batch of letters arrived for the prisoners, although there were none for Margot. The delivery did much to cheer the women and to reassure them that they had not been forgotten by their family and friends. On the same day, by pure coincidence, another Allied plane dived over Palembang and then rose majestically into the clouds. In October, the prisoners were all moved back to Muntok.

On 8 April 1945 they were moved again, this time to Loebok Linggau, for the Kempeitai still ruled supreme. Loebok Linggau was hidden in the jungle and was renowned throughout the Indies for being the malaria capital of the region. Without mosquito nets and anti-malaria drugs it was obvious that many would succumb to the disease:

In April 1945, we were brought back to the mainland. This meant a 60-mile trip up the river where we always managed to kill a few people because they were so weak and couldn't stand it. Then the camp we went to was way out in the jungle and no one could find us. I mean – we always said that they [the Allies] would never find us there.[11]

As Margot stated, this particular journey upriver killed a number of prisoners and amongst those for whom the journey became the last straw was the inspiring missionary Margaret Dryburgh. On 21 April 1945 Margaret died of fever and exhaustion and was one of the first to be buried in the new but obscurely located camp. Her loss was devastating for the other women whom she had cajoled and encouraged through the long desperate years.

The women were also convinced that the Kempeitai were making plans for their demise. These fears were not without foundation. Unbeknown to them, the Kempeitai had already compiled a long list of names in preparation for their execution. The women, however, had gathered together in their committees to discuss a way of fighting back should the need arise. They began to collect big stones while they were working and during their wood-collecting parties, storing them in secret hideaways about the huts.

They attempted to make rudimentary weapons, sharpening long, strong sticks and adapting kitchen equipment. But in reality, with the best will in the world, these primitive weapons were unlikely to offer any of them any real protection from the rifles and machine guns of the Kempeitai.

Notes

1. H. Frei, *Guns of February* (2004), p. 11.
2. Imperial War Museum Oral History Interview with Dame Margot Turner, ref. 9196.
3. Dame Margot Turner, extract taken from P. Starns, BBC Radio 4 Frontline Females Series, April 1998.
4. Testimony of Hak-Soon Kim, quoted in C. Enloe, *Maneuvers: the international politics of militarizing women's lives* (University of California Press, 2000), p. 80.
5. Frei, *Guns of February*, p. xxvi.
6. Dame Margot Turner, extract taken from P. Starns, BBC Radio 4 Frontline Females Series, April 1998. Also quoted in J. Smyth, *The Will to Live* (1970), pp. 95–6.
7. Enloe, *Maneuvers*, p. 215.
8. Ibid. p. 223.
9. *New York Times*, 7 January 1945, excerpt from from President Roosevelt's message to Congress.
10. IWM Oral History Interview with Dame Margot Turner, ref. 9196.
11. Ibid.

10

Congsi System

Despite the replacement of Hei Hoes by the Kempeitai, prison camp women still had some limited control over their own lives. The ways in which this control was exercised, however, differed to some extent between nationality groups. From the very first day of their internment Dutch internees had preferred to cook and organise their daily routines in extremely large numbers, whereas the British and Australian women adopted what became known as the congsi system. A congsi operated in much the same way as a family unit, and the number in each congsi varied between sixteen and twenty women and a few children. The definition of a congsi was also extended to incorporate groups of women who gathered together for a specific purpose. Within the concept of a hierarchy of skills, congsi formation was a crucial development that provided women with firm foundations from which to administer camp affairs. Congsi leadership was rotated to give each person a taste of responsibility and members formed a barrier of secrecy and protection for its members. This protection was particularly vital for vulnerable groups such as children, the elderly, the sick and those women who had witnessed Japanese atrocities during their capture. Australian nurse and friend of Margot, Vivian Bullwinkel, fell into the latter category.

Vivian was a survivor of a ship named the *Vyner Brook*, along with thirty other shipwrecked nurses, but when she arrived in the camp it was clear that something was seriously wrong. Margot recalled with restrained anger why her congsi members believed that it was crucial to protect this young nurse:

When Bullwinkel arrived it was hoped that she might be able to give news of the other Australian nurses. She walked quietly in through the door clasping an army water bottle to her side. We could see at once why she was doing this – it was to hide a bullet hole in her uniform. She had a most terrible tale to tell.

With thirty Australian Army sisters, a group of servicemen and civilian women she had reached the shore, some of them in the leaking life boats, at a beach about two or three miles from Muntok. They spent the first night sitting round a fire and then, next morning, as some of the men were wounded, they went in search of someone who might be able to care for them. However, they could find no one all that day so they spent another night on the beach. Next morning a naval officer volunteered to go off to try and get some stretchers and some food – and the civilian women went off on their own to find help. The Australian sisters, with Matron Drummond of the thirteenth Australian General Hospital in charge, stayed to look after the wounded. A little later the naval officer returned, bringing a party of Japanese soldiers with him. The Japanese separated all the nursing sisters from the men, and took all the men who could walk. They marched them along the beach and around the promontory. After a little while the Japanese came back, wiping the blood off their bayonets. They then formed the nurses and wounded into a line and told them to walk into the sea and machine-gunned them from the back.

All were killed except Vivian who was shot through the body and left floating unconscious in the water. When she came round and the Japanese had gone she struggled ashore. She wandered into the jungle and fell asleep. Next day she came across an English serviceman who was one of those who had been bayoneted. He was very badly wounded and Vivian stayed with him for several days, going each day to a native village to get water for him. The natives were too frightened of the Japanese to help them further, but they told Vivian about our prison camp and how to get to it. Eventually a Japanese officer picked them up and took them to jail. The English serviceman died a few days later.

What a terrible ordeal this young nurse had gone through and what tremendous courage she had shown. We decided in the camp that we would never mention this incident as, if it got to the ears of the Japs, Vivian's life might have been in danger.[1]

There were others in the camp in similar situations and women closed ranks around these individuals in order to safeguard them. They shielded their wounds from prying Japanese eyes, and often assumed responsibilities for their laborious chores around the camp in addition to their own. Once recovered from their ordeals the vulnerable women, along with their protectors, helped with the smallest and most cherished group of prisoners, the children.

There were three groups of nuns in the camp and two groups were qualified teachers. Between them they organised a varied school curriculum and the children were taught mathematics, English, French, geography, history and art. During the first two years of captivity children also benefited from teachers with needlework and craft-making skills. Footballs were made from pieces of canvas that were stitched together and stuffed with coconut fibres and dried leaves; rag dolls and other soft toys were constructed in a similar manner. Chess pieces and boards were painstakingly carved from wood, and for Christmas special gifts were made using sample books of silk, obtained on the black market from a cloth merchant. Gradually, however, black market supplies of foodstuffs, cigarettes, cloth, soap and other small extras dried up completely.

In some respects the camp was home to a baby boom and throughout the three-and-a-half-year internment period a number of babies were born in the camp.[2] Some of these were the result of emotional, loving and tearful farewell sessions between husbands and their wives before the fall of Singapore, whereas others were the result of clandestine liaisons, forced or otherwise, between prisoners and guards. A few women experienced miscarriages, and some chose to terminate their pregnancies rather than bring a child into the living hell of Japanese rule. Distressing and very painful terminations were effected by the administration of a foul concoction of elm and other herbs, which were supplied on the black market by native women. In other instances, cherished and deeply desired babies were sometimes stillborn because of poor nourishment and disease. Babies born healthy were often featured in Japanese propaganda photographs, designed to show the 'hospitable' nature of Japanese prisoner-of-war camps to the outside world. There were also children who tragically died in captivity having known no other life. Yet surprisingly the children were very resilient, partly because they were encased in a protective and remarkably altruistic female network. Margot stated: 'The Hei Hoe guards were, on the whole, good with the children and would perhaps offer them a sweet now and then.'[3]

The Hei Hoes were actually very fond of children and treated them well. They were particularly kind towards pregnant women, occasionally giving them extra food once the pregnancy had progressed further than three months. It was a common Japanese belief that the spirit of a baby entered a pregnant woman's body at twelve weeks, and later, when the camp came under Kempeitai rule, Commandant Siki took great pains to explain this belief to medical personnel. Margot recalled that the children were a constant source of surprise and an enduring cause of hope for their mothers:

It is amazing really how those children stood up to it. We didn't lose a lot of children. A lot of people died in the camp, but not a lot of children and some were very young when they came in. Those who were born in the camp had never seen anything of normal life. When the black market chap used to come with a horse and cart they used to rush to the fence with excitement. Most of them were only little tots when they entered the camp and probably about four or five when they went out. Some were born in the camp and knew nothing else, but they didn't run wild or anything like that. Sometimes they tried to play with the wild cats and dogs. Of course they couldn't be normal children under the circumstances but they were generally well behaved. I think, on the whole, the children survived quite well. They played together and were not troublesome as I can remember, but the boys did have to go to the men's camp when they were twelve.[4]

The heart-rending scenes of mothers desperately trying to hang on to their male children as they were forcibly removed from their clutches at the age of 12 by Japanese guards became a familiar sight as the years of internment wore on. Not knowing if they would ever set eyes on their children again, many of these distraught mothers turned their faces to the wall. But there were also examples of mothers who were so determined to be reunited with their sons that they battled courageously against hardship and disease, fuelled by that singular goal.

During the initial stages of internment children exhibited the same liveliness, enthusiasm, creativity and curiosity as normal children. But as disease, hard labour and deprivation began to claim more and more lives, they too became as despondent as the adults. But they did at least retain some physical strength. Indeed, towards the end of 1944 children were doing most of the grave-digging, since they had slightly more energy and stamina than the adults who had hitherto protected them.

Nevertheless, the congsi system had served the prisoners well. In addition to its mutual protection and community benefits, it also acted as a basis for industrial and economic endeavour. Women in Margot's congsi produced sun hats, fans, mattresses, clothes made from rice sacking and nuns' habits, and wooden shoes. Another congsi provided hairdressing, sewing and cooking services. This hive of industry was the mainstay of the prisoners' community and in the early years provided an exchange and barter system for food and other essentials on the black market. The congsi also allowed for some experimentation with cooking, since it was possible to try out new recipes on the family units before recommending them to others.

The British and Australian prisoners were housed on a different side of the compound to the Dutch, and the difference was clearly indicated by a number of congsi cooking fires located outside the British huts. In many ways they were reminiscent of Boy Scout campfire evenings. In order to keep the fires alight, the services of women nicknamed fire flappers were required. The wood collected for the fires was often wet, or running with rubber sap, and flames needed to be coaxed into life and constantly fanned to maintain momentum. Women spent considerable time and effort experimenting with fire-flapper techniques to ensure the best and most efficient methods for keeping it alight.

In the absence of men, women were no longer required to conform to previously held notions of femininity and most discovered new levels of resourcefulness. The nuns in particular became masters of do-it-yourself work and proved to be extremely good electricians. Art teachers became architects and planned new drainage systems for the camp; Margot headed the wood-cutting squad and became creative with the use of timber. She also used the trips outside the camp to plan thieving expeditions, whereby a number of nurses would follow Margot's lead in filling their wood sacks with vegetables from the gardens of Japanese guards. As Margot stated:

> A prisoner of war camp is no place for a goody two shoes. It was important to make good use of every opportunity to get vital food supplies. We were working very long hours on a starvation diet; we needed to grab anything we could get to eat.[5]

Margot and her close friend Netta always volunteered to help with the difficult jobs. These were often jobs that nobody else wanted to complete, but their congsi motto was 'someone has to do it'. They continued to clean the latrines and drains of maggots and rats, but also took control of constructing boundaries to prevent the overflow of toxic effluent from a nearby cesspool, and erected a wooden device that could carry cans of water efficiently. Women such as Margot were inventive, creative and capable. The prisoners rallied round each other in the congsi by giving emotional, physical and psychological support. Deprived of normal social systems, they created a democratic political framework that, in many respects, was amazing to behold. Faced with seemingly insurmountable problems on a daily basis, they refused to simply lie down and submit to their fate. Instead, they attempted, albeit haltingly at first, to establish some semblance of community life. Within a few months they had established a hierarchy of skills, camp sick bays, an efficient hygiene system, children's schools, an entertainments committee, religious services and a choir, mattress-making services and ration distribution networks. Their efforts did not merely demonstrate a will to survive; they clearly indicated a determination to derive some snatches of happiness, humour, love and community spirit from the ruins of their deplorable situation.

Most importantly, the congsi system represented their best survival tool, as the creators of the BBC series *Tenko*, Lavinia Warner and John Sandilands, revealed:

> The congsi was a definite statement of trust and reliance between its members, the submerging of sometimes unyielding individuality with which many women began the experience of the camps. The concept of a family was accurate and all the women remembered fondly those moments when they found strength from having cast in their lot with others at a time when such trust could literally have made the difference between life and death.[6]

In fact, all the survivors claimed that living in the camp opened their eyes to the real value of life, the importance of love and friendship, the will to live and the amazing beauty of life and freedom.

Margot later conceded:

> The experience taught me an awful lot about life and people. I do not complain as much as I used to before the war. I just take things as they come. But it was always difficult to know what was really going on, and each time we moved camp the Japs used to say that things were going to get better, but they didn't, they always got worse. You couldn't trust anything they said.[7]

One of the most difficult aspects of camp life was the uncertainty generated by the prevalence of rumours and riddles. Some of these rumours were started by the Japanese guards deliberately; they were an attempt to undermine prisoner morale and pre-empt any possible acts of rebellion. Margot always maintained that the British saying 'actions speak louder than words' held far more resonance than persistent rumour-mongering. With this maxim in mind, therefore, she realised before most of the others the implications signalled by the move to Loebok Linggau.

Margot's fears were well founded and Allied prisoner-of-war lives were indeed now at risk. But as they prepared to be ensconced in their malaria-ridden hell, hidden in the depths of the new jungle camp, rumours spread thick and fast. Bad-tempered Japanese guards began to shuffle about with an air of unease and irritability, while prisoners increasingly pondered their uncertain fate. A prisoner counterattack committee had already been established to prepare for the worst case scenario, but it was clear that some of these efforts would prove futile. Their only hope was to be discovered and liberated by Allied forces, and the women increasingly and earnestly looked to the skies for signs of a potential Allied victory.

Notes

1. Dame Margot Turner, verbal extract from P. Starns, BBC Radio 4 Frontline Females Series. Incident also recorded in J. Smyth, *The Will to Live* (1970). Smyth's account of this story cites a figure of twenty-one nurses rather than thirty, but War Office records confirm that the latter figure of thirty is correct. The Banka island massacre involving Vivian Bullwinkel became renowned as one of the most inhumane acts of the war.

2. The exact number of babies born in Japanese internment camps is not known, partly because records were destroyed and partly because some babies were stillborn due to poor dietary intake. The number of British children in Margot's camp when internment began was thirty-eight.

3. Imperial War Museum Oral History Interview with Dame Margot Turner, ref. 9196.

4. Ibid.

5. Ibid.

6. L. Warner & J. Sandilands, *Women Behind the Wire* (1982), p. 186.

7. IWM Oral History Interview with Dame Margot Turner, ref. 9196.

11

Riddles and Rumours

he last exhausting move for Margot and her fellow captives
had prompted a plethora of new and sometimes outlandish
rumours. But it was apparent to them that most of the time even
the Japanese Kempeitai were unsure of their fate. They simply
and unquestionably followed orders that filtered down to them through
the ranks of Japanese generals and army officials. These orders supposedly
complied with the wishes of Emperor Hirohito. Women who had gleaned a
little of the native language over the years attempted to eavesdrop whenever
possible, and they remained convinced that the guards were as much in the
dark about the state of the war as they were. Margot was also certain that
nobody had the faintest idea what was happening:

Various rumours used to filter through the camp. I think sometimes
deliberately started by the Japanese. On one occasion they said 'Buckingham
Palace has been bombed and all the royal family have been killed'. But
we wouldn't believe these things, though we always felt that perhaps
there was a bit of truth in it, and of course years later we did hear what
happened.[1]

It was amidst an atmosphere of general confusion, subdued anticipation and weary anxiety that prisoners embarked on their last but most lengthy and arduous trip across the humid Malayan landscape. Their destination was a place named Belalau, situated beneath a mountain range in Loebok Linggau on the furthermost western side of Sumatra.

First impressions of the Loebok Linggau camp were surprisingly favourable to the women who had trekked over 60 miles upriver to Palembang, then had been taken by a filthy coal train to Sumatra and loaded into dirty, overcrowded cattle trucks for the final leg of the trip that took the prisoners deep into the jungle. During the three-day journey prisoners who were already suffering from severe exhaustion, dysentery, scabies, beriberi, malaria and malnutrition were forced at the point of fixed bayonet to endure further misery. There was very little water en route and no food for the last twenty-four hours of their journey. Interminable Tenkos were conducted at random along the way as stony-faced guards struggled to keep track of prisoner numbers. Women who had reached the end of their tether collapsed as they attempted the required humiliating bow of submission for their captors.

The strong aroma of urine and excreta, mixed with the pungent smell of dead goats, permeated the train carriages and trucks, as weary prisoners covered in coal-dust grime endured the horrendous journey to their last camp. Six women died in the early stages of the trek and a further six women died in the cattle trucks only hours before reaching their destination. The new and well-hidden camp was low lying and a gushing river ran directly through the compound. Since it was surrounded by banks of beautiful, lush green tropical plants and flowers some women even gasped in amazement at the favourable appearance of their new residence. But Margot and a few others felt a deep sense of unease:

> The last camp we went to was way out in the jungle and no one could find us. It was near a rubber estate. I mean, we always said that they [the Allies] would never find us. It looked beautiful but it was very damp and there was a huge problem with malaria. The nuns were still with us and we continued to help them. By this time, of course, there were very few of us nurses left, even the robust Australian nurses were dying. I think by the end of it all there

were only twenty-four Australian nurses left out of the sixty-five that left Singapore in 1942.[2]

As the prisoners settled into their new camp it became clear that initial impressions were very deceiving. The river running through the site was heavily polluted and, because the women had rushed to bathe in its seemingly clear-running water, there developed sudden new waves of waterborne diseases. Wooden huts were surrounded by muddy banks which hampered food collection and the compound construction left a lot to be desired. Latrines had been built above the creek so all of the foul effluent flowed into the deceptively appealing river. This excrement was then combined with that of the Japanese guards, whose accommodation was located upstream. Prisoners were ordered by the guards to eat the riverside ferns, but supplementing their diet with these plants was not a sensible option. A young Australian nurse named Blanchie recalled the dangers of the riverbanks:

> The shoots on the ferns were lovely to eat. In this little creek there were some shell fish like periwinkles. We collected some and boiled them. We ate a few. Then along comes this doctor, and she had seen us getting these things, and said that if we got ill after eating those things she would not treat us. We didn't do it again. You see, the toilets were over this creek above us, and you can imagine what was in there. But we were so hungry we'd eat anything, though I don't think that any of our girls ever ate the rats.[3]

The small prison huts were situated in a low-lying gulley and the camp was infested with all manner of vermin. One event occurred at this time, however, which made the women think that divine intervention was at hand. An extremely violent thunderstorm and unremitting heavy rains resulted in the river bursting its bank; water gushed downwards and flooded the little huts, but along with the water came an abundance of fish. It was an event that stimulated conversation for some time, since there was enough fish for everyone to eat. Generally the women were kept awake night after night by the sound of heavy rains and falling tree nuts, since all huts were constructed with a corrugated iron roof. But despite these inconveniences, all the women noticed a general atmosphere of change from the middle of 1945 onwards. The guards appeared to be adopting a more relaxed approach and a few even managed a smile! Tenkos became less frequent and hut inspections were less rigorous. In many respects the altered mood was unnerving for the women, as Margot noted:

> We knew something was happening because at one stage the guards brought sixteen pigs into the camp and we were allowed to kill and eat them. Then a few days later we were ordered to go to a concert. We were almost taken there by fixed bayonet! None of us wanted to go but when we got there it was lovely. They played all the music we knew. We thought that they [the Kempeitai guards] must have been reading regulation something or other on how prisoners of war were supposed to be treated [laughs].[4]

Whilst the women would have liked some regular food, medicines, soap and a few other basics, the concert was, in fact, a remarkable gesture to the internees. But it was with some degree of nervous anticipation that the women gathered in the compound and sat in the shade of the rubber trees to listen to a thirty-strong Japanese band and a few singers. Music consisted mainly of Austrian waltzes, popular German tunes and classical overtures. Stony-faced Kempeitai guards informed the prisoners the following day that they were all required to write thank you letters for the concert. Similarly, they were given postcards to send to relatives with the words already chosen for them; all they had to do was put a signature to the card. The words extolled the kind hospitality they had experienced as prisoners of war, and highlighted the benevolence of the Japanese guards. Most women chose either not to sign the cards, or they signed with a pseudonym.

No sooner had the prisoners recovered from their impromptu concert than more news from the outside world infiltrated the camp. A further two batches of letters arrived for the women and, although heavily censored, a few Australian letters mentioned the word 'demobbed', which sparked further rumours about the state of the war.

But death rates had accelerated rapidly amongst the prisoners since their arrival at Belalau and an increasing number of women no longer cared about rumours or the state of the war:

Out of sheer weakness scores of prisoners died in these last months of captivity. Many of the children were in a terrible condition, some of them so badly affected by beriberi that they could hardly walk. The hospital hut was full and the nursing sisters found it very hard work. Malnutrition was making itself felt to an increasing extent. Quite a lot of time had to be spent in making patients eat. We would sit for hours trying to make them take even half a teaspoonful every five minutes. If they refused to eat at all they very soon died. It was very grim and exhausting nursing – particularly as some of us sisters were in need of nursing ourselves. On the long wooden benches in the hospital, which served as beds, the patients lay cheek by jowl.[5]

The despondent prisoners were unaware that the war in Europe was over. Furthermore, they had no knowledge that Allied offensives and the American blockade of Japan, which had denied Japan the raw materials to make weapons, were taking their toll on the Japanese Imperial Guard. Allied bombing raids on mainland Japan that had been stepped up from the beginning of 1945 had made distinct signs of progress, much to the relief of Australian government ministers, who had firmly believed that Australia was next on the list for a Japanese invasion.

As soon as the American forces had captured Okinawa and Iwo Jima, Allied air raids were again increased. However, although the Allies were fighting the formidable Japanese and winning, it was clear that the latter would never surrender. Even in the face of certain defeat no Japanese official would take the decision to surrender, because he would then have to be executed for dishonourable conduct. The code of conduct for all Japanese warriors was known as bushido and stated that it was better for a warrior to die at the hands of the enemy, or indeed to kill himself by committing hara-kiri, than to suffer the shame and humiliation of defeat. Confronted with this intractable code, Allied commanders took a monumental decision and dropped the first atomic bomb on Hiroshima. Margot remembered the huge impact of this event:

There was a real hullabaloo and the guards seemed visibly upset and then one day, one of the guards said to one of the Dutch women that there had been a very big bomb somewhere but not in Sumatra, and that was all we knew.[6]

The guards were seriously disturbed by this dramatic turn of events and their irritability increased. Some guards even committed suicide in the prisoner-of-war camps, believing that this act was more honourable than facing a trial by enemy forces. Various descriptions of the bomb circulated around the camp, and were obtained by women who had been over-friendly with the Japanese guards. Observers had reported seeing flashes of extremely bright blue light which then turned into a series of rippling yellow rainbows, and they all noted with astonishment an overwhelming blast and wall of intense heat that radiated across the landscape. The effect was total carnage. An area of 47 square miles was completely flattened. The devastation was immense and the fall-out even greater.

But the decision to use the atomic bomb had not been taken lightly. British commanders were worried about the safety of Allied prisoners of war, believing that without a Japanese surrender all prisoners might be killed. American politicians, meanwhile, highlighted the potential economic implications of a drawn-out conflict and the political and strategic benefits of using atomic weapons. American commanders were worried about the massive number of troops that might be lost in combat if the war became a prolonged affair, and believed that the atomic bomb would force an unconditional surrender from Emperor Hirohito. Scientists too had an agenda, largely based on curiosity. Nobody knew for certain quite how much devastation could be caused by the atomic bomb. Japanese refusal to surrender gave them an ideal opportunity to test this new weapon of mass destruction.

The first atomic bomb was uranium based. Nicknamed 'Little Boy', it was dropped without warning on Hiroshima at 8.15 a.m. on 6 August 1945. It weighed 9,000lb, and was transported by a B-29 Superfortress piloted by Colonel Tibbets. Despite the horrific consequences of this action, surprisingly, the Japanese still refused to surrender. Three days later the Americans dropped a second atomic bomb on Nagasaki. This bomb was plutonium based, and nicknamed 'Fat Boy'. The shocking combined death toll from both bombs was estimated at 240,000, and thousands more suffered the effects of radiation sickness.

On 15 August Japan capitulated and Emperor Hirohito gave a radio broadcast to his people to inform them of his surrender. He signed unconditional surrender terms with Mountbatten on 29 August 1945 and with MacArthur in Tokyo Bay on 2 September 1945. The latter had invited General Percival, who had been forced to sign the humiliating surrender of Singapore to the Japanese only a few years earlier in February 1942, to attend the official Japanese surrender which took place on the battleship USS *Missouri*. This venue was specifically chosen because, by sheer coincidence, the ship bore the same name as the birth place of the new American president. As thirty-third president, Harry Truman took over from President Roosevelt following his death in April 1945. He became a highly respected leader, particularly in the field of foreign policy. Furthermore, he rigorously defended his decision to use the atomic bomb against the Japanese on the grounds that ultimately its use actually saved more lives than it destroyed.

Following the Japanese surrender, it became obvious that the British fears for the fate of Allied prisoners of war were well founded. They were also running out of time. One by one the jungle camps were located, and in each camp there was a detailed list of prisoners who were all destined for execution by firing squad.

As Margot noted, it was clear that the woman and children of her camp would not have survived without Allied intervention:

> They [the Japanese] were going to get rid of us. They found papers in the camp. We often wondered if they were going to line us up and shoot us or what they were going to do. I subsequently learnt that, if they [the Allies] hadn't had the atom bomb, we had eight days to live – that we were all going to be annihilated in groups. [The Allies] found all the lists. So I must say that the atom bomb saved a tremendous lot of Allied prisoners' lives.[7]

Undoubtedly the Allied decision to use atomic weapons and their resultant devastating consequences prompted a considerable amount of worldwide political and public controversy. But their use had also granted Allied prisoners of war a last-minute reprieve. Nevertheless, the road to freedom for the incarcerated women and children was not straightforward. Javanese nationals had reacted to the Japanese surrender broadcast by declaring an immediate 'Republic of Indonesia'. Huge banners proclaiming their independence were hung from all available buildings and fences, and fighting broke out in the streets. The Javanese nationalist movement threatened violence, particularly against the Dutch, and although they longed to escape their Japanese oppressors, Margot and her fellow prisoners were forced to remain in the camp until Allied assistance arrived:

A week after the [Pacific War] was over we were sent for. The commandant told us that the war was over and we were no longer enemies but friends. He advised us to stay where we were for our own safety. The men from the camp a few miles away came to see us. They would come over in the day and do all the heavy work for us, but they still went back to their own camp at night. We never saw their camp but it was a couple of miles up the road I think. But the Allies couldn't find us. Some Japanese said they would come back and drop food and medical supplies, which they did. Then a young South African who came over after the war said he was sure there was another camp. He kept persisting that there was another camp of women and children and they did eventually find us, but not until the 10th of September. We were the last camp they found. They were just about giving up I think.[8]

In total, 230 Japanese prisoner-of-war camps were located. During a period of six weeks, and covering an area that stretched 3,000 miles through Burma, Siam, Malaya, Sumatra and Java, 90,000 prisoners of war and other internees were rescued. The official recovery organisation was known as RAPWI (Recovery of Allied Prisoner of War and Internees) and was administered from a relief co-ordination centre in Singapore. Medical officers and nursing sisters from military hospitals in India and Ceylon were amongst those who worked with the relief services. Many of the camps were almost impossible to find without prior knowledge of their existence because they were hidden in jungle terrain and were well camouflaged.

Japanese guards, fearing Allied retribution for the maltreatment of their women folk, had taken somewhat bizarre measures to make it appear that the women had been well treated. Each woman was given a toilet roll, which they immediately nicknamed their 'victory roll', and a bright red lipstick. Moreover, as the Allies approached frantic guards ordered the women to wear the lipstick in a desperate attempt to improve their somewhat jaded appearance. In reality, the garish lipstick only succeeded in making the women look like clowns, by highlighting their white, pasty and malnourished skin.

Red Cross food parcels were suddenly and miraculously released from storage and the women were bombarded with tea, sugar, butter, powdered milk, bandages, vitamin pills and medicines such as quinine. One of the most welcome products was soap. Mosquito nets were also hurriedly distributed and extra rations were delivered daily by the truck load. Released men from the male prisoner-of-war camp helped the women with heavy work, such as tree cutting, and made trips into the jungle to hunt and kill wild pigs and deer. For the first time in three and a half years prisoners were getting enough to eat. There were no more humiliating Tenkos, no more sleepless nights or lying in fear of being chosen as a Japanese plaything, no more carrying water for their afternoon baths and no more struggling to find food.

On 10 September a South African officer named Major Gideon Jacobs was parachuted into Margot's camp. He had organised an air delivery of food and medicines and he explained the need to wait for further Allied forces. As they awaited their deliverance the women of Belalau were encouraged by Jacobs to write down their experiences. All of these experiences were carefully documented and collated along with those that were recorded in other camps. They subsequently provided much of the evidence for the war crimes trials.

Eventually aeroplanes began to arrive on a regular basis and to begin with they airlifted the very sick, since they were a priority. One nurse who vividly remembered the relief and rescue efforts was Gertrude Ramsden, member of the Queen Alexandra's Royal Naval Nursing Service and personal nurse to Lord Louis Mountbatten:

Even before the surrender ceremony, already seeing the appalling conditions in the prisons, the Royal Air Force flew leaflets, medical supplies and food to known camps. Immediately 'Sister Ann' the Dakota flew Lady Louis and her rescue team thousands of miles. This historical tour of prisoner of war camps was life saving. Lady Louis at first accompanied by the Director of Medical Services and a secretary were dependent on the Japanese for the location of the camps. They met thousands of starving men, bringing them food, medical supplies and hope for their release. She had the authority and fortunately the Japanese did as they were told. Her untiring efforts speeded up the rescue operations ...

In mid September the other Royal Navy sister named Lucy and I were flown in a Sunderland to Singapore having offered to help. On arrival Lady Louis suggested we report to the military hospital which was crowded with ex-prisoners of war. There I helped to nurse over one hundred and thirty Indian troops, all in one ward and suffering from advanced tuberculosis; Lucy was caring for civilian patients, who were mentally and physically ill as a result of their internment.

On the 28th September we flew with six Red Cross welfare workers into Batavia. There we saw the handful of British officers, helped by ex-prisoners of war, administering a city using Japanese troops. They were doing guard duties as willing subordinates. We were then taken to Tjideng camp to meet those who were caring for the sick and wounded in an improvised hospital. The horror of seeing over nine thousand Dutch women and children crowded together, with over a hundred in each bungalow had to be seen to be believed. Suffering from general malnutrition, wasted and scantily clad, anxious for news and still hungry, they found us a novelty.

I still don't like the Japanese. I am afraid I am not a Christian. I will not buy a Japanese sewing machine. Some of them were very nice. Our interpreter was a Japanese Christian and some of them were very charming. So I think there are good and bad in every nation. I still think that the Emperor made a very truculent speech at the end of the war and I must say that I do not go out of my way, but I like to keep away from the subject, I think it's best.[9]

Margot and her friend Netta, who had helped her clean the drains and latrines and had accompanied her on all her vegetable-thieving parties, were taken from the camp on 18 September:

We went from the camp as we had come – in Japanese open trucks. We had the same Japanese truck drivers who had been so insolent to us when we arrived; now they were offering us sweets and butter would not have melted in their mouths. On the train journey to Lahat the Japs, who had treated us like cattle before, were coming round with curry, but we had brought our own rations and had the satisfaction of refusing their offers. What a thrill it was when we arrived at the little aerodrome and saw the aircraft, which was to take us back to liberty and civilisation, appearing over the hills, and then landing. It was my first experience of air travel and not the most comfortable as there were no seats and we all sat on the floor. But what did anything matter? We were leaving a hateful place and a terrible experience behind. We arrived in Singapore on the 19th of September.[10]

On arrival in Singapore Margot and Netta were accommodated in the luxurious Raffles hotel – a place they had fondly remembered and often dreamed about during their years of captivity. For the following seven days they revelled in their surroundings, enjoying small comforts such as a real mattress, a mirror, a proper bath, sweet-smelling soap and new clothes. Margot also noted the excitement that encompassed the newly released children at that time:

> They were so excited. They had never seen so many buildings or traffic. Some had been so very young when they came into the camp that they'd never seen a bus or anything like that. They were running around everywhere with real delight and fascination.[11]

Most of the children had never seen any form of transport other than the rickety old cart that was pushed by the black market trader who positioned himself outside the camp each week, and the dusty old truck that had dumped their food rations onto the road each morning. The experience of seeing so many different forms of transport, shops, parks and ornate buildings in Singapore was a total joy for the little ones, some of whom had known no other life but the barbed-wire compound and dingy huts.

Following some relaxation and respite care, Margot and Netta left Singapore on 26 September and set sail for England on a Polish ship named *Sobieski*. They arrived at Liverpool dock on 24 October, where Margot parted company with Netta and stayed for one night in a military camp to undergo a medical examination. Margot's parting from Netta was very emotional, since both women had shared so much. From dirty jobs such as the cleaning of maggot-filled drains to teasing the Japanese guards; from sharing humorous stories of their nurse training schools to coping with harrowing disasters; from catching a random cockerel to confronting their many life and death experiences, Margot and Netta had travelled a unique and uncomfortable road together. Their combined emotional strength and close friendship had sustained them through the most traumatic and horrific circumstances and they had lived to tell the tale. They were stoical survivors of a cruel and barbaric regime. The British Nursing Journal reported in December 1945:

All women who have had the privilege to wear the uniform of a trained nurse hail with sincere rejoicings that noble band whose release from a murderous crew of inhuman wretches comes after three and a half years of imprisonment, yet who face life with unbroken and unquenchable spirit. The revolting brutalities perpetuated on helpless white enemies, men and women alike, show so similar a pattern of sadistic bestiality that the system must have been originated by those who held power in Japan. We hear of the thirty Australian nurses who were machine gunned to their death while still in the water, wading ashore after their ship had been torpedoed. The revelations coming in from day to day of callous torture, of electric current playing on wet nude bodies, of strenuous, continuous work on starvation diet among malaria infested country, will make everyone who refuses to face the issue, acknowledge that the Japanese race is sub-human, beyond the pale of civilisation.

To the lasting honour of those few nurses who have survived among the sixty-five who were evacuated from Singapore, February 1942, just before it fell, they retained their courage and integrity, their desire to help those worse off than themselves, their sense of decency and humour during unspeakable mental and physical privations. The epic story may be related as a whole; in the meantime one must be satisfied to receive it piecemeal. Never has the uniform of a member of the nursing service earned such well deserved credit as it has in innumerable instances in the tragic tumult of 1939 to 1945.[12]

Notes

1. Extract from P. Starns, BBC Radio 4 Frontline Females Series, April 1998.
2. Imperial War Museum Oral History Interview with Dame Margot Turner, ref. 9196.
3. Testimony of Jessie Eaten-Lee (Blanchie to her nursing friends) of the 2/10th Australian General Hospital, interviewed on 6 May 1998. The testimony can now be found at www.angellpro.com.au/Blanchie.htm.
4. IWM Oral History Interview with Dame Margot Turner, ref. 9196.
5. Ibid.
6. Ibid.
7. Ibid.
8. Ibid.
9. The recollections of Gertrude Ann Ramsden as told to the late Dr Monica Baly and entrusted to the author. 'Sister Ann' was a Dakota plane belonging to Lord Louis Mountbatten and named after Sister Ramsden.
10. J. Smyth, *The Will to Live* (1970), p. 125.
11. IWM Oral History Interview with Dame Margot Turner, ref. 9196.
12. The British Nursing Journal, December 1945.

12

Regaining Confidence

T he fall of Singapore had provided, perhaps, the first indication
that the old British Empire was collapsing. Some government
ministers had even used the island's capitulation to suggest the
abolition of British public schools: 'It has been said that the
Battle of Waterloo was won on the playing fields of Eton. I do not know
by analogy, we ought to say that the Battle of Singapore was lost on the
playing fields of Harrow.'[1]

The bitter disappointment voiced within official British circles and the
national press highlighted deep concern about the potential loss of global
influence and colonial territory. American politicians had outlined their
plans for self-determined small countries in accordance with the Truman
Doctrine, and encouraged democratic rule by implementing the Marshall
Aid programme. American Marshall Aid gave money to European countries
that were badly affected by the trauma of war to help them rebuild and
reconstruct their cities, schools, hospitals and administrations; more
importantly it also helped them to resist Communist takeover. America also
became part of a crucial peacetime military alliance with Europe under
the auspices of the North Atlantic Treaty Organisation (NATO). Indeed,
the international post-war world emerged as a very different entity to the

pre-war colonial world, and America and Russia were now the deciding global forces.

The loss of colonial territory and accompanying global influence was a bitter pill for British government ministers. Many were ashamed about Singapore's dramatic and largely undefended capitulation during the war. Thus the relatives of British survivors and nurses like Margot were told not to meet them off the ships in Liverpool docks. Ministers did not want their homecoming to attract any media attention, lest the whole abysmal episode of Singapore be dragged through the press again. Therefore, Margot's arrival at Liverpool docks in September 1945 was a subdued affair, almost an anticlimax.

This was in stark contrast to the gleeful parties and homecoming celebrations that awaited Australian nurses and survivors of the Far East prisoner-of-war camps. They were greeted with large cheering crowds, colourful bunting flags and tables heavily laden with food, laid out in the streets. Fortunately for Margot, an understated welcome was more in keeping with her temperament and her expectations. She was never one to want a fuss or lavish attention. Gaunt-looking, with skin tinged yellow from vitamin deficiency, a raging tooth abscess, a limp from a time when a tree log fell on her leg, and a need to find some peace and quiet after the years of incessant chatter and barked orders, Margot simply wanted a nice cup of tea and a soft, warm bed to sleep in at the end of her journey:

I always said that I would never buy anything Japanese, and I would always have two of everything and one for the wash. When it came to clothes, I mean, one to wear, another in the drawer and one in the wash. That plan didn't last long. I couldn't get much in the way of clothes just after the war anyway, because there were still clothing coupons, you know, rationing was still around. But they [British army personnel] looked after me very well after the war. On my return my face and body was very bloated, I had rice belly I think, but it didn't last for long. They fed me very carefully and I could not eat meat for a while. Once or twice I had a fever when I was home. One didn't feel well and did not have much strength. But I recovered well.[2]

Margot subsequently underwent a series of medical examinations and was then sent on extended leave to be reunited with her family. She managed to spend Christmas with her mother and catch up with old friends. In the meantime, her younger brother Peter set out to discover why his sister had spent six months in Palembang prison. Now a British Army major, Peter demanded some information with regard to his sister from the Japanese 25th Army Divisional Headquarters at Pandang.

The reply he received was a poorly concealed attempt to fob off his legitimate enquiries. Japanese officials claimed that there was absolutely no record of Margot's prison spell whatsoever, and no record of any other nurse by name. They did reluctantly issue a brief and carefully worded statement about the doctor and his wife, who were arrested at the same time as Margot and interned alongside her after they had been tortured. The report was dated 18 December 1945 and read as follows:

With Regard to British Nurse E.M. Turner

We have been ordered by HQ 25th Army to investigate the reasons why the above-named person was interned in a prison for six months from April 1943. We have tried to find the truth of the reasons why the above-named person was interned in prison during the said period but because of the lack of papers referring to and also being unable to locate the exact persons concerned in this incident we regret that we are unable to produce fuller reports. Nevertheless we report herewith an incident similar to the one asked.

Dutch medical doctor and wife – Hall Waige [spelling uncertain because of translation] and nurses (names unknown):

The above named having professional standings as doctors and nurses were, by their wishes and under pledge (whether all of the dually [sic] sweared or not is uncertain) released from confinement in the early part of 1943 to serve on the staff of the Palembang Residency Hospital.

In April 1943 at the time of an anti-air drill, they did nothing whatever to heed the orders to darken the lights of the hospital though warned to several times. Therefore, Mr Waige and wife who were in charge of the hospital were called in for questioning. They were not only unable to explain the reasons for not carrying out the orders but displayed antagonistic emotions and furthermore showed no signs of wishing to co-operate with the civil administration. Summarizing along with their daily activities, they were charged with the suspicion of communicating with the enemy as well as breaking the rules and regulations of a Released Hostile National and forthwith interned for further investigation.

The local prison under the supervision of the civil police being for natives, it was seen as both unwise and unfit to have them interned along with the natives where sanitary conditions were bad. Therefore they were placed in another internment house under Japanese control. They were not treated as ordinary prisoners and given many privileges, such as receiving food from without and the possession of anything they wished. The other nurses upon the internment of the doctor and his wife refused to remain at their post at the hospital and asked that they should be returned to the internment camp. They were, like the others, under suspect of also communicating with the enemy and, as a means of preventing espionage, were interned along with the others. After carrying out various investigations no definite evidence could be found to confirm the charge of the above stated suspicion and also of their change of attitude were released and sent to the internment camp in September of the same year.[3]

Although this report did not specifically mention Margot by name, it is likely that she was one of the nurses referred to in the statement. However, the dates do not match exactly those recalled by Margot, and the accounts of treatment are a work of pure fiction. Nevertheless, given the clandestine activities of the nursing nuns and other hospital staff, it was clear that Margot was simply an unwitting and innocent victim of circumstance. She had simply got on with her work as a theatre sister, whilst all around her were busy passing radio messages, letters and medicines to resistance workers and others who opposed Japanese occupation. With her practical, professional devotion to her patients, and working within the primitive operating theatre with its basic surgical instruments, Margot knew nothing of the undercover world of espionage that had embroiled the hospital and many of its inhabitants. For her, the period of her prison internment alongside murderers and thieves remained a perplexing mystery until her death. She stated with conviction during the recording of her oral history testimony that she did not have any inkling of what she was supposed to have done wrong, and there was an air of resignation in her voice as she admitted that she would probably never know. There were a good many other people in Margot's situation, all of them innocent bystanders who were caught up in the intrigues of others. Margot had survived better than most because she was determined to focus on the future rather than bewail the privations of the past.

Three and a half years in captivity had taken its toll on all the prisoners of war. A number of them still suffered the effects of tropical diseases and an even greater number suffered from the psychological trauma of being held in such proximity to others for a prolonged time. The institutionalisation process had clearly affected Margot and had created a certain number of subsequent habits, which she attributed to camp life. The first of these was the habit of speaking her thoughts aloud whenever she was alone, or when she was writing letters. During her time in captivity there had been so many times when it was impossible for her to 'hear herself think' – times when she was forced to speak out loud above the chatter of the other women simply to clarify her thoughts. The legacy of this time in the crowded camp compound produced a seemingly automated and conditioned response when she was alone and deep in thought. Sitting on her bed writing letters to friends or family members she would speak her thoughts out loud, and this was sometimes pointed out to her by visiting guests. The second and understandable habit was borne of the deprivation experience. All food and supply cupboards were always full to the brim. Thus Margot stockpiled tinned fruit, vegetables and meat. She also hoarded other essentials such as soap, toothpaste, toilet rolls and washing powder: 'I would explain to those who visited me, that there had been a time in my life when I had been very short of everything, and I vowed that I would never go short of anything ever again.'[4]

Though she rarely spoke of her time in captivity after the war, it was clear that Margot had suffered in the same way as many of her fellow prisoners. Nevertheless, her nursing and military training had stood her in good stead and evidence from all camps suggested that nurses were better than most at picking up the pieces of their fragmented lives and getting on with things. Margot had proved to be more mentally and physically resilient than some of the others in her camp. But readjusting to a life of freedom was not an easy process for any former prisoner of war. There were women who had grown so used to being surrounded by others that they experienced extreme terror at the thought of being on their own. There were also those who suffered badly from agoraphobia and were unable to even go to a post office to buy a postage stamp. Others were terrified at the thought of going to visit a doctor or dentist. Everyday, normal activities, such as walking to the shops, riding a bike in the country or going to the cinema, were simply out of the question for a large proportion of these women. One nurse survivor remembered her period of readjustment as slow and painful:

> The first few days I wanted to feel like a human being. I found it extremely difficult in one way because I was so nervous, having been hemmed in for so many years behind barbed wire, always surrounded by hundreds of people, and longing for a bit of privacy but, when it came to it, I found it was very difficult. I was alright in my brother's house and his wife was very sweet and kind, but I was afraid to go out by myself, I was afraid to answer the telephone. When I went to the shops for the first time I couldn't ask for what I wanted and I had to come out again. I went to the post office and couldn't think what I wanted. I found it most difficult.[5]

The years of deprivation and humiliation had taken their toll but in many respects the survivors were undoubtedly the lucky ones, since many had been massacred, tortured or brutally murdered. War crimes trials were held in Tokyo under the administration and supervision of Australian Judge William Webb. Other trials were convened in Singapore, Hong Kong and a few smaller cities. In total, the International Military Tribunal for the Far East lasted for a period of 417 days. One of the nurses who gave testimony at the Tokyo trials was Vivian Bullwinkel, the only nurse survivor of the Banka island massacre. Her wounds had been hidden from the Japanese prison guards and she had been cosseted and protected by Margot and others in her congsi just for such an important day – to bear witness for her fellow nurses who had not survived. Vivian later travelled across Victoria, Australia, with another ex-prisoner, Betty Jeffrey, raising public awareness of the massacre and collecting funds that enabled them to establish an educational memorial centre in Melbourne in honour of these fallen comrades.

As the tribunals continued, other prisoners described their horrific journeys and the inhumane treatment they received as they travelled between different camps. Tribunal judges were faced with a seemingly endless list of barbaric acts and tortuous incidents. Consequently, during this time over 900 people were sentenced to death, often for crimes that had been committed against civilians of occupied territories.

One civilian woman, who was accused by the Kempeitai of helping Resistance workers, reported to the court in February 1946:

> My young daughter was hung from a tree about ten to twelve feet high, under which there was a fire. She remained suspended there while I was tied to a post nearby and beaten with a stick until it broke in two. Sergeant Yoshimira kept shouting to me to speak out, but speaking out, as I and my daughter well knew, meant death for hundreds of Resistance people up in the hills. My child answered for me. 'Be very brave Mummy, do not tell. We will both die and Jesus will wait for us in Heaven above.' On hearing these words I told the Sergeant that he could cut the ropes and burn my child. I told him that my answer was 'no' and that I would never tell. All I can remember is that as they were about to cut the rope God answered my prayer. A Japanese officer who had arrived on the scene took pity and ordered the Sergeant to take down my child. She was sent home and I was sent back to my cell.[6]

Twenty-five Japanese military leaders were tried and found guilty in Tokyo and seven of these received the death sentence; the remainder received custodial life sentences. Strangely enough, the Japanese Emperor Hirohito was not tried for war crimes. The consensus of official Allied opinion seemed to conclude that Hirohito had been something of a passive bystander of events and had not been responsible for the Japanese expansionist plans, military strategy or subsequent massacres; he was nonetheless forced to relinquish all claims of having divine status. Thus a 'non-divinity' clause was written into the official surrender document. The Japanese war minister, extreme nationalist and later chief of staff, General Hideki Tojo, was tried as a Class A war criminal, since it was he who had devised military strategy and given the orders for massacres. He had effectively established a dictatorship in terms of his command by monopolising all influential posts. He did, in fact, unsuccessfully attempt suicide in September 1945 when the American forces captured Tokyo, but he was forced to stand trial instead and was executed in December 1948.

Alongside the acts of punishment and retribution there were also amazing acts of forgiveness and reconciliation. The bishop of Singapore, for instance, the Right Reverend John Leonard Wilson, was brutally tortured by the Kempeitai during his wartime captivity but he resumed his Christian ministry work as soon as he was released. One of the first people he baptised on his release was one of the Kempeitai officers who had directed and taken part in his torture. The bishop also refused to be repatriated, despite his poor state of health, preferring instead to stay in Singapore in order to help organise refugee aid and relief networks. His overriding theme of work throughout his remaining years was that of forgiveness. He argued that without forgiveness of the enemy, bitterness ensued and consumed people. General Percival, who had been forced to sign a humiliating surrender in 1942, subsequently and tirelessly devoted his post-war years to constructing and assisting the Far Eastern Prisoners of War Federation to help and support ex-prisoners of war.

As a devout Christian, Margot adopted a similar approach to that of Bishop Wilson, and she believed that it was important to forgive, though not necessarily to forget:

> I feel towards the Japanese the same as I feel towards anyone else. I mean, the generation now had nothing to do with the war. It is very important not to hate people, because that's how wars get started.[7]

Aside from the need to come to terms with war issues and reconcile their feelings, the ex-prisoners of the Far East often had problems that had not confronted those who had been confined in Europe. Many of them still suffered with tropical diseases, for instance, and the long-term effects of malnutrition. Most of those who had spent such a painful and despairing time in captivity no longer knew how to pick up the threads of their lives, and some were apt to suffer severe and recurring bouts of malaria. Moreover, there were more broken marriages amongst the ex-prisoners of the Far East than in any other prisoner-of-war group. Perhaps this situation arose because so many husbands and wives had lost all hope of ever being reunited with their loved ones and had switched off their emotional connections. Undoubtedly some were simply unable to communicate their feelings again because their experiences of torture and deprivation had rendered them emotionally bereft. Margot had counted herself lucky in that she had not married since this was one less problem to worry about. Her concerns had been for her mother back in England and her brothers, who were also in the armed forces.

The period of readjustment for ex-prisoners extended to their comprehension of how events had unfolded during the war. They had been cut off from the rest of the world for such a long time in the camp that they had no idea of how various battles had been fought and won; they had no knowledge of life on the Home Front and no understanding of why certain political changes had happened. As Margot stated:

> We were all astonished to find that Churchill was no longer prime minister after all he had done for us in the war – truly astonished. It seemed inconceivable to us that somebody else was voted in. We had no idea of what was going on – there was a batch of letters in 1944 but otherwise no news at all, and I am still waiting for my letters. I also sent some post cards, two from the camp and one from jail, but they never arrived. My family are still waiting for them.[8]

Despite all his valiant and inspirational leadership during the war, the British people rejected Churchill and his Conservative Party and overwhelmingly voted for change in the immediate post-war era. This change came in the shape of Clement Atlee, leader of the Labour Party. There appears to be a consensus of opinion amongst historians that Churchill was rejected because he did not offer a post-war construction plan to the British electorate. Churchill had headed a wartime coalition government in which all parties had some input in policy formulation. Undoubtedly he was a strong and committed leader throughout the war, but there were many who believed that he might rest on his laurels in peacetime, although it can be argued that the number of social reforms that were introduced during the war would indicate that this would not necessarily have been the case.

By the end of the war, government efforts to improve public welfare, for instance, had borne considerable fruit. There were fewer cases of childhood diseases, fewer deaths from influenza and childhood mortality was dramatically reduced by the vaccination of children against diphtheria. Improved access to milk and food had resulted in a greater resistance to infection generally, and in many respects a welfare system of sorts had already evolved by default, long before it was formalised by government legislation. During the war Lord Beveridge had been given the task of identifying the root causes of poverty and recommending measures to combat it. His subsequent report identified the problems of want, disease, ignorance, squalor and idleness, and outlined the ways in which these could be tackled to encourage a healthy and economically productive British population. His assessment of social problems and, more importantly, his comprehensive system of social security based on a National Insurance scheme became the 'blueprint' for the post-war welfare state and encompassed a vision of a new and prosperous future for the British people.

When the Beveridge Report was first published in 1942 people queued round the block in order to get their hands on a copy of his recommendations. Moreover, it was clear that most people embraced his concept of social change and believed that the Labour Party was more likely than any other to initiate this change. This belief more than any other was responsible for the rejection of Churchill.

Under the rule of Atlee, the National Health Service was introduced and a series of educational and social reforms were implemented. Many of these were based on the Beveridge Report that had outlined a system of social welfare benefits designed to care for the population from the cradle to the grave. The Butler Education Act of 1944 had already brought about educational reform and raised the school-leaving age. A Children's Act was also put into action to provide better protection and welfare for children.

Amid the onslaught of sweeping social changes on a national level, there were significant adjustments made within the international arena. A decolonisation process was in full sway and India was given independence in 1947. The new post-war superpowers were America and the USSR and an arms race prompted the subsequent era of Cold War politics. Britain continued to maintain a special relationship and firm alliance with America.

As British society entered a period of substantial post-war reconstruction, individuals were busy picking up the threads of their lives. There was an acute labour shortage and women were increasingly urged to enter the workforce once again. Between 1946 and May 1955 the number of married women in gainful employment rose by 2.25 million, to 3.75 million.[9] The British government had attempted to resolve labour shortages by immigration alone, but this policy had not entirely bridged the gap. Although not all employed married women were mothers, concerns grew over the plight of latchkey children, and local authority officials became preoccupied with an increasing number of problem families.

While civilians came to grips with the aftermath of war, military personnel were entering a period of reconstruction. Demobilisation was slower than many expected, partly because of the lessons of the First World War, when a sudden influx of too many men into the civilian job market had contributed to an economic depression, and partly because British military commitments across the globe had not diminished. Military commitments to the North Atlantic Treaty Organisation and within the Middle East ensured an increasing demand for troops, despite the establishment of National Service. Military medical and nursing commitments also continued to grow and Margot was to prove a crucial component within this process.

Margot had always been a strong, capable and straightforward woman but the camp experience had taken its toll on her confidence levels. Her identity and life commitment had been to the civilian and then military nursing profession. Nursing was her life and vocation, but in the aftermath of her dreadful experiences in the Far East she had lost confidence in her professional skills and knowledge. Medical developments had moved swiftly during the war and Margot was deeply concerned that they had left her behind. Yet it was through her military nursing career that Margot regained her overall confidence to face the future.

Military personnel understood more than most the physical and mental trauma that Margot had suffered as a result of her shipwreck experiences and subsequent internment. They also knew her character more than most, and how to deal with her professional fears. As far as they were concerned Margot was, and always had been, an excellent and efficient theatre nurse. She was also an undoubted heroine and was awarded the MBE in February 1946 and the Pacific Star medal in recognition for her bravery.

In the same year, once she was cleared for duty by the army medical board, Margot was deployed to Horley to work with surgeon Colonel Marsden. The latter deliberately threw Margot into the deep end in terms of theatre work and she adapted and rose to the challenge very quickly. Together they dealt with a number of difficult and complicated operations but, as she worked in her familiar nursing environment opposite Colonel Marsden, her self-assurance returned. He recalled their working relationship as follows:

> When Margot Turner came to me I already knew something about her prisoner of war background, including the terrible privations she had suffered while she was adrift on the sea for some days. I was a bit of a perfectionist in the theatre and a specialist in both general and orthopaedic surgery. When she joined my theatre staff she told me that she had forgotten most of her theatre technique, but I told her that once you have learnt to ride a bicycle you can always ride a bicycle, no matter how long you have been away from it. I deliberately plunged her into the deep end as a Theatre Sister opposite me in all varieties of operations, from the relatively minor, for example, hernia, to the major ones, for example, bone grafts, and I deliberately took the attitude that she was an efficient Theatre Sister who knew her job. Certainly there were a number of minor corrections that had to be made, such as recalling to memory the names of different instruments, but, other than that, provided I worked at a slower pace than usual, she was able to keep up with me, and at the end of a week the atmosphere of being 'lost' was quickly replaced by confidence, and she became in a very short time one of the most efficient Theatre Sisters I have ever had. Perhaps the re-birth of her confidence in herself and in her relationships with the world in general was generated by the handling of her professional duties in the operating theatre.[10]

By September 1946 Margot had been promoted to captain and was subsequently sent to Windsor to study administration. This new course in administration and management was established specifically to enable the armed forces to train their own nurses. Hitherto, nurses were trained in the civilian sector and then entered the military, if they so wished, once they had passed their state registration examinations. But during the war, officers decided that a military nurse training course that would conform to the standards of the civilian General Nursing Council was infinitely preferable to the rather haphazard training standards of individual hospitals. Besides which, in terms of medical development and nursing practice the civilian sector was significantly behind its military counterparts. The military, henceforth, organised their medical and nursing practice on a 'brick' system and specialist teams, whereas civilian nursing still conformed to an outdated and sometimes inappropriate system that had not really changed much since the days of Florence Nightingale. Furthermore, whereas reports compiled by Sir Robert Wood and Dr Cohen attempted to reform civilian nursing by introducing educational as well as practical training, military nursing had already moved forward in this sense, as Dr Cohen acknowledged:

> Nor can I sympathise with the view of the chairman Sir Robert Wood, that 'at best the progress of reform is bound to be slow'. The rate of reform will rather depend on the will to act. The services have shown what can be done where the will exists to initiate and swiftly execute vast new training programmes.[11]

There was also a distinct shortage of nurses at this point in time, a problem of major concern in view of the forthcoming National Health Service. In 1947 a Mr Isaacs at the Ministry of Labour announced in the House of Commons that 'October last my department had particulars of over 32,000 vacancies for nurses and over 6,500 vacancies for domestics, most of which were in hospitals'.[12] This acute shortage of nurses was relieved in a number of ways. Between June 1945 and December 1947, 19,651 female nursing members were released from the armed forces nursing services.[13] All military personnel were offered quicker demobilisation if they agreed to embark on a nursing career and special rates of pay were introduced. Intensive one-year registration courses were reluctantly established by the General Nursing Council 'to encourage more men and women who have had substantial nursing experience in the Services to make nursing their career'.[14] Members of the civilian General Nursing Council had rather arrogantly stated that ex-service nursing orderlies would find intensive registration courses too difficult; in fact, examination results did not bear out these assumptions since the number of passes – 91.1 per cent – exceeded the normal pass rate for nurse training.

As more hospitals relied on recruitment from the armed forces for their nursing staff, many of them established strong links with ex-servicemen's associations specifically to aid the recruitment process. Enterprising matrons set off for the Caribbean to recruit nurses from the Commonwealth. But the fluctuations in the standard of nurse training varied dramatically across the country, and certainly between the old local authority hospitals and those more esteemed voluntary hospitals. This variation, and the fact that military medical needs differed somewhat from those of civilians, prompted the military to establish their own nurse training schemes. Even those military nurses who left the armed forces at the end of the war to nurse in civilian hospitals found the transition difficult, primarily because the latter were outdated in nearly every sense.

In some more amusing incidents it can be argued that there was quite literally a war of the wards! Military nurses would eagerly get patients out of bed following a hernia operation, for example, after a period of three days, whereupon civilian sisters would rush to put the patients back to bed, insisting that they could not be moved for at least two weeks. Obviously military nurses knew that the said patients could be moved earlier and survive, because they had done so during the war. This example and others of medical change were lost on civilian sisters.

Medical specialities had also developed during the war, such as physiotherapy and occupational therapy. Advances and specialist units within military medical services were, and remained for some years, streets ahead of those that could be found in civilian services. Thus Margot was sent to learn systems of administration to enable the military nursing services to train their own, uniquely equipped personnel.

The Queen Alexandra's Imperial Military Nursing Service was renamed as the Queen Alexandra's Royal Army Nursing Corps. This change reflected the recognition of the army nursing service as a corps in its own right and its adherence to the army rank pattern. A new military nurse training centre was established at Hindhead on 13 September 1950. The QAs were also afforded their own 'march past' tune entitled *Grey and Scarlet*, which was designed to emphasise their role as soldier and nurse and to fit in with military tradition. Furthermore, the status of military nurses continued to outstrip civilian nurses, and this was reflected in the recruitment statistics. The British Nursing Journal announced:

> We learn that while hospitals are finding great difficulty in recruiting nurses, applications greatly in excess of vacancies are being received by the nursing services of the Royal Navy, Army and Royal Air Force. All these nurses are granted officer status. Travel and distinctive uniforms are further attractions. Only 109 of the 455 nurses applying can be accepted by the Queen Alexandra's Imperial Military Nursing Service, as the service is being reduced from the peak wartime figure of 12,000 to its normal complement of 624. For 11 vacancies in Queen Alexandra's Royal Naval Nursing nearly 60 nurses are competitors.[15]

New military administration systems were necessary to train nurses to meet the necessary requirements at Hindhead. Much as Margot found the administration course dull and rather irritating, she later acknowledged that she learnt a great deal. It was not unusual for Margot to slightly resent any training activity that took her away from nursing and the task at hand. Nevertheless, as she ascended the ranks there were times when other tasks were necessary. In May 1947 Margot was sent to the British military hospital in Intarfa, Malta, and later that year she went to Benghazi. Here she resumed her sporting activities, such as riding and tennis, in her off-duty hours.

> We were kept so busy and were so understaffed that I used to occasionally relieve the theatre sister and always made myself on call for the theatre in case of emergency. I enjoyed keeping my hand in at a form of work in which I had formerly specialised – before my captivity.[16]

The major advances in blood transfusion technology enabled surgeons to embark on pioneering techniques in the operating theatre, especially in the field of transplant surgery. Margot kept abreast of all these new innovations in addition to her increasing administrative duties. There was no doubt that her character, intelligence and natural leadership shone through as she worked and she soon became a leading light in the military nursing profession. She worked hard and always put the needs of others before her own:

> To begin with I didn't see the point of all the administrative courses, but as the Corps was restructured and we began training our own nurses from scratch, I could see why they were needed. Then I was suddenly sent on temporary duty to the British Military Hospital in Benghazi, where the sister in charge had had to go home on urgent leave. This was the first time I had ever been to Africa. We had half an Italian hospital, which was on the outskirts of the town of Benghazi. Our Mess and Sisters' Quarters were across the road, opposite the hospital, and we had little bungalows with two Sisters in each. The Mess was hutted and the bungalows brick built. The hospital was supposed to be a hundred bedded, so we were very understaffed with only twelve Sisters. We had to put extra beds up, though, as we always had more than a hundred patients, who were all from British troops stationed in Benghazi. There was also a small hospital in Tobruk, with three Sisters.
>
> We had the ordinary medical and surgical cases, road accidents and normal routine sickness cases that one always gets in a military hospital. We were certainly kept very busy but I found time to play quite a lot of tennis on the court attached to the Mess, and at the Officers' Club. And I started riding again in Benghazi. The horses weren't very good but an Army Riding Club was formed with the local ponies and of course there were plenty of places in which to ride.[17]

From Benghazi, Margot travelled to Cyprus in December 1948, then to Cairo. By this stage she was almost wholly involved with administrative work, and was required to travel extensively. She had never liked flying but forced herself to get on aeroplanes, just as she had forced herself to eat rice during her internment:

> I always preferred to travel by ship but sometimes one does not have a choice. I had worked in six different countries in three years and it was inevitable that I would be required to do a lot of travelling, so I had to fly. I had considerable

difficulty getting to Cyprus. I had to go by air from Benghazi to Port Said, where I caught a ship to Famagusta. My plane was held up in Tobruk and I eventually arrived in Cyprus about a week before Christmas 1948. The British Military Hospital was in Nicosia. It was a very old hutted building with a large wing for Jewish migrants to Palestine. They were accommodated in an encampment outside Famagusta.

The Jewish wing had some of its own nurses, but our Matron and Deputy Matron used to visit it and their surgical cases came to our operating theatre, of which I was in charge when I first went there. Our Matron was Colonel Somerville and the Deputy Matron, Major Agnes McGeary, was the very famous QA who had accompanied the Chindits in Burma. I remained Theatre Sister for two months; then the Matron was posted home, Major McGeary became Matron and I became Deputy Matron. I was still a Junior Commander with three pips. In April 1949 I was again detailed for temporary duty in Egypt – at 211 Transit Camp, near Ismailia on Lake Timsah on the Suez Canal. All QAs who were posted to Egypt came through the Transit Camp before joining their various hospitals and all of those going home went through there too. Although the job was a temporary one, I took all of my luggage with me, as some of these temporary jobs had a habit of becoming very lengthy affairs.

Ismailia was certainly a nice place and we had good quarters but I never liked Egypt or the Egyptians. However, since I had to be there I made the most of it. I went to Cairo, saw the Pyramids and toured up and down the Canal. I was the only QA in the Transit Camp so I was kept fairly busy; but of course the work was entirely administrative.

About this time, a Sergeant in the Argyll and Sutherland Highlanders, who was an ex-prisoner of war of the Japanese had had a bad car accident and was lying seriously ill in a field hospital in Aqaba. British Military Hospital was asked if it could supply a Sister to nurse him and the Principal Matron asked me if I would go. I was delighted at the thought of doing some nursing again and accepted gladly. I set off immediately for Aqaba in a large plane all to myself and sat with the pilot as we flew across the Sinai Desert. The field ambulance was in tents and they were certainly pleased to see me. They fitted up a room for me behind the little operating theatre. I was the only Sister there – in fact, I was the only white woman in the place. I nursed the

Sergeant for a week until he was well enough to be moved and then I flew back with him to the British Military Hospital at Fayid.[18]

There was no doubt that Margot had gradually regained her confidence and enthusiasm for life. But the internment period had left her with some health problems, including a reduction in her resistance to infection, and she succumbed to pneumonia in 1952. Subsequently invalided in a military hospital, it took several months for her to fully recover. Superior officers decided that she had probably been working too hard and she was posted to Tidworth following her recovery. Here Margot entered the Medforth Lawn Tennis Championship and won – such were her extraordinary powers of recuperation.

In 1953 she was shifted back to Kingston, where she was given command of the QAs designated to take part in the Queen's Coronation Parade. In order to prepare her QAs for the honour, Margot took them around the route every weekend and they rehearsed at every opportunity. In total, the parade ground course stretched over 13 miles. Starting at Buckingham Palace, they marched to Birdcage Walk, on to Constitution Hill and Hyde Park Corner, through the park grounds to the imposing Marble Arch, down Oxford Street and into Regent Street. Every corps and regiment was represented during this extremely disciplined parade, and it was a great honour for all participants who were chosen. The rehearsals grew more frequent and intense, all uniforms were inspected meticulously and the nervous QAs found it difficult to contain their excitement.

Coronation Day itself was very sunny and hot. Margot and her QA contingent marched with pride and enthusiasm, in unison along with other military personnel, in an honourable act of homage and affiliation to their newly crowned monarch. By the end of the day they were all exhausted from marching and standing to attention in the sweltering heat, and most, including Margot, chose to retire to bed early rather than enjoy the evening celebrations. Nevertheless, Margot firmly maintained that taking part in this ceremony was a magnificent opportunity and Coronation Day was the greatest and most fulfilling day of her life. She was duly awarded the Coronation medal and felt a wonderful sense of satisfaction at a job well done.

Notes

1. Hansard, House of Commons Parliamentary Debates, 5th Series, 16 June 1942, col. 1431.
2. Imperial War Museum Oral History Interview with Dame Margot Turner, ref. 9196.
3. J. Smyth, *The Will to Live* (1970), pp. 85–7.
4. IWM Oral History Interview with Dame Margot Turner, ref. 9196.
5. Extract from P. Starns, BBC Radio 4 Frontline Females Series, April 1998.
6. L. Warner & J. Sandilands, *Women Behind the Wire* (1982), p. 162.
7. Ibid.
8. Smyth, *The Will to Live*, pp. 136–7.
9. R. Titmuss, *Essays on the Welfare State* (1950), p. 102.
10. Smyth, *The Will to Live*, pp. 136–7.
11. Dr Cohen, The Minority Report on the Recruitment of Nurses, p. iv, HMSO, 1948.
12. Hansard, Parliamentary Debates, 5th Series, vol. 445, 20 November 1947.
13. P. Howlett, *Fighting with the Figures* (1995).
14. National Archive General Nursing Council files: DT/16/585.
15. The British Nursing Journal, 1946.
16. Smyth, *The Will to Live*, p. 141.
17. IWM Oral History Interview with Dame Margot Turner, ref. 9196.
18. Ibid.

13

Ascending the Ranks

Within the field of British military nursing Margot had proved her leadership skills beyond any doubt. She possessed a quiet air of authority and a deep sense of integrity that encouraged the young to emulate her strength of character. Throughout the many changes in nursing and medical practice, systems of administration, military locations and political upheavals, Margot maintained a constant and dignified sense of direction. She successfully steered her nurses through a veritable obstacle course of post-war reconstruction, and never lost sight of her core values and belief systems. It was also clear to her that preventative medicine was the key to future healthcare delivery, but while military medical personnel understood this fundamental truth, the civilian medical field failed to come to grips with it and curative treatment continued to take precedence. This problem was highlighted by articles in *The Lancet*:

> The more medical people get to know of the cause of disease, the more those diseases can be avoided. Of the £439 million spent on the National Health Service, £238 million has gone to hospitals and a mere seven per cent of the money went on the prevention of disease.[1]

Thus civilian healthcare networks did not consider the problem of keeping the population fit for industry, whereas the military medics had long realised that the soldier needed to be kept ready for battle. There were other incidences that highlighted divergences in the structure of civilian and military medical and nursing practice. Civilian nurses had adopted the concept of the military officer status for registered nurses but had failed to provide officer-style leadership. Therefore, civilian nursing stagnated while military nursing continued to progress. The financial differentials between civilian and military nursing had also widened considerably. In 1947 military nurses had a £46 per year lead over civilian nurses; by 1962 this lead had escalated to the sum of £239. Not surprisingly, many registered nurses were flocking to join the armed forces by this point. The wartime matron-in-chief, Dame Katherine Jones, had achieved her aim admirably; by making sure that her nurses assimilated to the army pattern, she had successfully assured their status and pay structure. Throughout the 1960s and '70s, therefore, while civilian nurses were beleaguered by poor working conditions, low morale and political unrest, military nurses relished their *espirit de corps*.

Military medical personnel had recognised that most recruits consisted of two distinct personality types: those who preferred to have decisions made for them and those who wanted to take part in the decision-making process. Military officials had concluded that the armed forces needed to cater for both personality types. Some recruits, they argued, were capable of producing independent ideas within contemporary society, but initiative and self-reliance in others was stultified by the all-providing welfare state.[2]

As senior military personnel acknowledged, in terms of professional advancement it was important to encourage the 'thinking personality', while simultaneously providing an adequate environment for the characters who were 'content to have everything done for them'.[3]

Herein lay the crux of the matter for civilian nurses. Although they had adopted the military model of nursing practice to some extent, they had only accepted the features that made for a compliant workforce. Civilian nursing had failed to cater for the thinking personality and thus an essential component of the military nursing system had been lost. Moreover, without this component civilian nurses were clearly unable to direct professional development. In both fields of nursing, however, staff were trained to deal with unexpected situations and clinical emergencies, and this training ultimately relied on strict and necessary discipline. As Dr Baly noted: 'In nursing, like the army, crisis tends to be normal and the operating theatre and the battlefield are notorious for not lending themselves to sweet reason.'[4]

Margot was familiar with both of these scenarios and was adept at disciplining herself and others. By now she was much travelled and had gleaned considerable medical knowledge. She had also been able to gain some relaxation and a renewed lease of life. Margot's brother and nephew were serving with their regiments in Hamburg while she was stationed there and she spent many happy hours in their company. From Germany she travelled to Bermuda, where she acquired the art of fishing. But her time in Bermuda was also tinged with great sadness as her mother died during the first year of her posting there.

A year later, while she was still working in Bermuda, Margot was awarded the Royal Red Cross medal, which was presented to her by Queen Elizabeth at Buckingham Palace in 1957. She was also promoted to major. Margot clearly led by example rather than by dictatorial methods, and her devout religious beliefs gave her added strength and the courage of her convictions. In 1958 her eldest brother suffered a fatal heart attack and she had only two brothers remaining. Despite this personal suffering Margot continued her work unabated. There were occasions, however, when she succumbed to bouts of ill health, particularly pneumonia. In one year she suffered two severe spells of the illness. Margot attributed this physical weakness to her period of internment.

By 1962 Margot was promoted to colonel and posted to Cyprus. By this stage she had travelled the globe and had steadily risen through the ranks of her profession. She had loved living in different countries, particularly Hong Kong, and had enjoyed visiting America. In March 1964 Margot was promoted to matron-in-chief and director of the British Army nursing service. Furthermore, she was appointed the Queen's Honorary Nursing Sister. Now Margot was responsible for all nursing in all military hospitals, including those situated within the Commonwealth countries. In stark contrast to the civilian nursing field, senior military nurses exerted considerable power and influence not just within Britain, but also in terms of contributing to the formation of international medical policy. In May 1965, for instance, Margot took part in the SHAPE medical conference, which was held in Paris, and the International Congress of Nursing, which was held in Frankfurt. All the North Atlantic Treaty Organisation countries were represented and all branches of the armed forces. This was the first time women had contributed to NATO talks and Margot stayed at the conference for five days before she embarked on a tour of military hospitals across Germany.

In June of the same year Margot was made a Dame of the British Empire in the Queen's Birthday Honours List. She was absolutely over the moon with excitement and her only regret was that her mother and eldest brother were not alive to attend the ceremony. Following the presentation, which took place in July at Buckingham Palace, Margot was posted to the Far East. This was an extraordinary experience since she was able to view Singapore in a new light. It was the first time she had revisited the island since her brief stay there after her release in 1945. The Alexandra Hospital and the officers' mess seemed untouched by the intervening years, but the old hospital at Tanjong Malim was now a college. There was a large British hospital in Penang and a huge aerodrome at Changi. Indeed, it was difficult to locate the old hospital at Changi amongst the array of new buildings. Raffles remained, but Margot felt that it had lost some of its former splendour. Compared to the new and more vibrant-looking buildings and hotels, Raffles seemed drab and dreary – a lack-lustre product of a bygone age.

On her return to Britain Margot worked hard to ensure the highest standards of military nurse training and embarked on a punishing inspection tour. One of her friends recalled the thorough nature of her hospital visits:

When inspecting a hospital as Matron in Chief Margot's main subjects of interest were in the general standards of the hospital, the nursing care of the patients, the welfare of the nursing staff and the training of other rank nurses. She usually spoke to every patient and interviewed any of the nurses who had asked to see her. During her visits there was generally a social occasion at which she could meet both the Royal Army Medical Corps and the QARANC officers informally.

After her retirement my husband and I continued to see Margot frequently. I remember one amusing occasion when Margot came to stay with us. I had made one of my favourite rice puddings, quite forgetting that Margot had had to live on rice for over three years. She ate it quite gracefully – and then said: 'That was very nice, but it isn't exactly my favourite sweet!'[5]

Margot rarely spoke of the dark days of war, but she had undoubtedly emerged from her ordeal with her strength of character and spirit intact. Major-General M.H.P. Sayers recalled Margot's dry sense of humour:

Margot was a tall, good looking girl and full of fun. She was a fair tennis player and fond of a party, but unfortunately I only knew her for a few months in Bareilly and I remember her mostly as a charming and dedicated nurse at the hospital. The war came and we went our separate ways, I to the Fourteenth Army and she to Singapore. I only heard vague rumours of her fate and did not see or hear any more of her until we met unexpectedly at the Royal Army Medical Corps sports at Aldershot, when the conversation went something like this:

'Hello Margot, I thought you were dead!'

'Did you Pat? I am sorry to disappoint you.'

She then went on to ask about my wife and family.[6]

During her time as matron-in-chief Margot worked extremely hard, and in addition to her formal military work she contributed to the policies of the International and British Red Cross and St John's Ambulance Brigade. The main QARANC depot was moved from Hindhead to the Royal Pavilion in Aldershot and the new training centre was opened officially by Her Royal Highness Colonel-in-Chief of the QARANC Princess Margaret, Countess of Snowden.[7]

Under Margot's leadership the military nursing profession had embraced education and professional development with open arms. As a consequence, senior nurses from the various nursing corps were among the leaders in creating what has become institutionalised as the Brussels-based Senior Women Officers Committee within NATO. At the time of its formation in the early 1970s, nursing officers were the highest-ranking women throughout North American and Western European forces.[8] By contrast, the civilian nursing field had been racked by political protest, threatened strike action and had a need for adequate and effective leadership. This lack of professional leadership prevented educational reform and training initiatives. Dr Baly pointed out:

> The process of democracy in (civilian) nursing was delayed because technical knowledge advanced with such rapidity that each generation was stranded on the beach of insecurity.[9]

Even the World Health Organisation commented that British civilian nurses were poorly educated. More surprisingly, perhaps, the chain of command between the matron-in-chief in the military sector and her subordinates was always intact. The formation of nursing policy was actually a more democratic process within military realms than in the civilian field. Each successive matron-in-chief paid as much attention to the views that emanated from below as to those that were imposed from above. In terms of professional autonomy and expectations, the experiences of civilian and military nurses were worlds apart. The latter were able to prescribe drugs, give intravenous injections and adopt leadership roles, while their civilian colleagues were still fighting to be allowed to take a patient's blood pressure. It says much for the excellent leadership provided by Margot during her time in office that standards of military nursing care were second to none at a time when British military overseas commitments were continuing to increase.

Notes

1. *The Lancet*, 17 November 1951, p. 935.
2. Royal Army Medical Corps, Field Training School Precis Gen 6-Man Management, p. 5, Wellcome Contemporary Archives, London: RAMC/1976/9/1.
3. Ibid.
4. M. Baly, *Nursing and Social Change* (1980), p. 81.

5. J. Smyth, *The Will to Live* (1970), p. 165.

6. Ibid., p. 8.

7. Please note that the QARANC Museum is also based at the Royal Pavilion, Aldershot. It is here that the compact Margot used to collect vital rainwater during her time on the raft in the Java Sea can be viewed, along with other items of memorabilia associated with Margot's life and that of other QA nurses.

8. C. Enloe, *Does Khaki Become You?* (1983), p. 114.

9. Baly, *Nursing and Social Change* (1980), p. 230.

14

This is Your Life

*D*ame Margot retired in 1968 and became the colonel commandant of the nursing corps. She continued to stay very active and spent a considerable amount of time catching up with her many friends.

During the 1970s a hugely popular biographical Thames television programme, named *This is Your Life*, chose to honour the life of Brigadier Dame Margot Turner. The programme was presented by Eamonn Andrews and followed a similar format each week. The subject of the programme was taken through the events of their life and reunited with people who had played a key part in their lives, and who recalled anecdotes and important issues along the way. The first time the producers tried to make a programme about Margot she discovered that something was afoot and put a stop to the whole process. However, Margot's friends were so distraught that they pleaded with the producers to make a second attempt at surprising Margot and highlighting her achievements. Thus, on 25 January 1978 Margot became the reluctant star of the television screen.

It was, by anyone's standards, a momentous and highly moving programme. Lavinia Warner was a young researcher for the programme at the time and it was her job to locate and reunite the survivors of Margot's

Japanese prisoner-of-war camp. She later recorded the atmosphere of the programme that entered people's living rooms across Britain on that cold, wintry Wednesday evening and documented her thoughts about the truly amazing women who were reunited:

> They were not young, nearly forty years had passed since the events they were asked to describe, but there was alertness and firmness in their manner that did not make age the first aspect of them that a stranger would notice. They tended to be conventionally dressed: muted colours, discreet fabrics, neat coiffures. You would not single them out except for that air of self possession. At every stage of the programme's preparation they tested politely but warily for any hint of extravagant attitudes or indifferent taste. They were there to pay a tribute to Margot Turner, whom they all regarded highly, and even an audience of some twenty million viewers was not going to tamper with their natural restraint.
>
> In the event, as the programme unfolded, they were admirable. They told their stories with brevity and humour then withdrew gracefully to take their places with the rest of the guests. There was no suggestion of the extraordinary revelation that was in the offing as the programme came to its end.
>
> The women had agreed to sing a hymn composed in the camps by a missionary who had died there. It was known to them as the 'Captives Hymn' and it had been sung at all religious services which had continued, against bitter odds, every Sunday until freedom came. Now this little group of survivors from those days gathered round Margot Turner and, unaccompanied as they had been then, and a little hesitantly at first in these strange surroundings, they began to sing. But as the words flooded back and their confidence grew there was a truly remarkable transformation. The years visibly fell away from them and the cloak of their reserve disappeared so that they were young women again, vulnerable, beleaguered, a little afraid but taking strength from each other as they must have done then.
>
> Sensing the uniqueness of the moment the camera lingered on their faces and through its insistence all were quite discernibly immeasurably distant in time and place from a television studio in central London and under the gaze of millions of strangers. It was suddenly apparent that an extraordinary sisterhood had existed between these women in those

days when they had faced a common peril together and had last sung the 'Captives Hymn' together.[1]

The reluctant heroine and star of the show, Margot was also deeply moved by this powerful reunion:

In our camp we had put up with each other, and of course we were great friends. On the whole we got on. It was wonderful on *This is Your Life* to see some of the people I had not seen since we left the camp in 1945. It all started again just like we'd seen each other last week or the week before, it was a wonderful reunion.[2]

The remarkable and powerful reunion prompted Lavinia Warner to conduct more research into the subject of women who were interned by the Japanese, and along with another producer, John Sandilands, she produced the highly successful and long-running television series entitled *Tenko*. However, while the nation was gripped by the series and tuned in each week in increasing numbers, Margot was unimpressed. When an official Imperial War Museum interviewer asked her if she thought the series was an accurate representation of her experiences, Margot was adamant:

No, I don't think it was. They had too many clothes for a start. Lots of things happened. For instance there always seemed to be lots of fighting and squabbling and we didn't have that sort of thing. They [the actresses] seemed to be too well dressed. But then one is apt to judge a thing by your own circumstances and your own camp. I was told that this [*Tenko*] could have been any camp where women were prisoners, it wasn't necessarily our camp. I didn't really watch it very much, it wasn't very interesting. There was so much that we didn't see you see.[3]

The dramatisation of *Tenko* charted the lives of several women, and although the producers had maintained that the portrayal of their internment could well be any camp, it clearly drew from Margot's experiences and that of other survivors from her camp. The series included Margaret Dryburgh's choir of voices, for example, and many other character representations drawn from real women's lives.

No doubt the process of dramatisation distorted camp life and events to some extent for the purposes of making an interesting programme. Arguments and an atmosphere of general discontent perhaps draw viewers in greater numbers than a story of women getting on well together and being supportive of each other. Nevertheless, it did not convey the strong and emotionally cohesive sisterhood that many women had experienced during their captivity.

Margot may well have disliked the programme because she did not want to mentally return to the living hell of her internment. But there may have been another reason for her hostility towards the programme, and this may well have been prompted by what she would undoubtedly have interpreted as misrepresentation of her character or that of military nurses in general. The only English nurse in the first series of *Tenko* was called Molly, and although it is not entirely clear whether or not this character was based on Margot, there were enough similarities in background and personality traits to make some viewers believe that this could be the case.

The character Molly was said to have been born and brought up in London, and she was portrayed as being a calm, stoical, supportive nurse, who was dependable with a cool head in crisis situations. All of these characteristics could be attributed to Margot. But as the series progressed Molly was given a storyline that indicated to the viewers in no uncertain terms that she had lesbian tendencies. According to the drama, Molly befriended a young woman who had just given birth to a stillborn child and then entered into a supposedly unnaturally close relationship with her. She thus became the subject of considerable prison camp gossip.

The *Tenko* series was highly acclaimed and very popular with the general public and undoubtedly this storyline intrigued the viewers at home; but in many respects it could be viewed as an outright betrayal. Margot had co-operated fully with the programme, and it was her own unique life story that had prompted the series. For producers to then portray the only English nurse with such overtly sexual overtones was not only totally undignified, but also potentially insulting. Margot had always had her full share of male admirers and the fact that she had chosen to dedicate herself to her career rather than get married and have children was purely a personal choice on her part. Margot was born into a generation of women that could not expect to have a life of domesticity and a satisfying career – it was either one or the other. Women's magazines reflected this dilemma. Some publications warned of the perils of independence, claiming that such self-sufficient women would be unable to find husbands and be destined for loneliness in old age. Other magazines openly championed career paths for women, and suggested that they were a feasible course of action even for those women who had chosen motherhood as their preferred option. Writing in the November edition of *Girls' Own*, one young woman stated:

> I would like to see almost every girl married. Even more fervently I would like to see her equipped for a career. Both offer different ways of enriching and fulfilling her individuality. Marriage and motherhood can, of course, be a whole time job, and the most selfless career in the world. But motherhood should be regarded as a temporary one, for the sake of the children as well as the parents.[4]

Whilst this *Girls' Own* writer was obviously expressing a future desire, in terms of the options that could potentially open up for women, without the necessary societal frameworks in place to support women's careers, a career path was not a practical consideration for many women during these early post-war years.

For Margot the decision was clear, since her first love was always for her profession. As a deeply religious person, Margot was committed to a sense of duty to God and to her country. All other concerns were secondary when compared to these commitments. During the early 1980s, however, when the BBC *Tenko* series was first screened, the options that were open to women were radically different to those that were presented to Margot in her earlier lifetime. It was perhaps very difficult for some television scriptwriters to comprehend why some women might have chosen a military career in 1945 in preference to raising a family. Even government ministers in 1945 seemed perplexed as to why women would choose to have a career rather than opt for a life of domesticity. They stressed that demobilised servicewomen needed to be helped back into a life of feminine grace and glamour; whereas the more knowledgeable and discerning military officers stated that women in the armed forces were more concerned about their future employment prospects than how they appeared when they looked in the mirror.

Government assumptions about women and their desire to return to traditional feminine roles were quite astonishing and restrictive. Mass Observation reports, however, had a clearer perspective on female choices and appeared to express a more realistic view of women in the military:

> Service women constituted a particularly restless group. They had rejected the idea of settling down, they had a longing for adventure and they desired change. Service women are, on the whole, much more interested in the future than their counterparts in factory and war jobs.[5]

In the supposedly more liberal post-war British society some people continued to find this choice remarkable. Gender constructions, in some respects, became more fixed as society struggled to return to pre-war values and structures. It was often women rather than men who expressed their discomfort and disapproval at members of their own sex who chose to go against the grain and opt for a military career. These attitudes demonstrated a lack of knowledge and understanding of what the armed forces could offer, and a total misconception of why women were attracted to them in the first instance. To make assumptions about Margot's sexual orientation, or indeed that of any other military woman, was potentially distressing and grossly insensitive. It is highly likely that the *Tenko* scriptwriters were simply trying to make an interesting story, and gave little thought to the potential repercussions or the feelings of those involved. Nevertheless, their portrayal of the only English nurse in the series left a lot to be desired. It is not clear whether or not Margot made a formal complaint to the BBC about this portrayal, but for whatever reason the character of Molly was dropped from the second and third series of *Tenko*.

In addition to recounting her experiences for the series *Tenko*, Margot was involved with some BBC documentaries that attempted to retrace her wartime footsteps and locate the various internment camps. She thus returned to Muntok and was reunited with the Charitas nuns. But as she later recalled, neither the journey nor the task was easy:

> I was asked by Ludovic Kennedy to revisit Muntok. We went in search of all the camps for a BBC omnibus programme. The road to Muntok was as bumpy as it always was, and it was a difficult journey. We tried to find all the camps but it was impossible to find the one in Loebok Linggau, there was no trace of it at all. But I met some of the nuns again when we went back, and quite a few of those who had been in the camp were still there.[6]

Along with the television producers and another survivor of the camp, Mrs Betty Jeffrey, Margot embarked on an emotional journey. She revisited the horrific Palembang jail, Palembang cemetery and the Charitas Hospital. She also discovered that the only surviving landmark of the prison-of-war camp in Muntok was the large stone well where they used to draw water in the heat of the day. Most of the other sites were overgrown and almost unrecognisable. It was impossible to find many of the graves that they had so laboriously dug for the women who had turned their faces to the wall so many years earlier. They had always marked the graves with small wooden or bamboo crosses and had usually made some attempt to carve the names or initials on these simple markers. But time had eroded all trace of such efforts.

By contributing to *Tenko* and subsequent documentaries about the women who were interned in the Far East during the war, Margot believed that she had gone some way to keeping the memory of those women alive. Most of them had no memorial. Until her return to Muntok, Margot's memories of her own ordeal had been kept hidden and secluded in a dark corner of her mind, and it was obviously uncomfortable to revisit and open old wounds. However, she did enjoy meeting Sister Catherine once more and they reflected on the war years and the history of Charitas Hospital together. Although she had nothing to outwardly show for her years in the Far East, Margot henceforth kept an enormous amount of memorabilia with regard to her travels and her ceremonial duties. Photographs of exotic countries and historical monuments featured strongly in her retirement home. She later claimed that her favourite places were Hong Kong, San Francisco and Bermuda, and her least favourite place was Egypt.

I found Bermuda a most delightful place and I loved every minute of my two years there; but I don't think I would ever want to live there and it does get an awful lot of tourists. I joined a woman's club, the Altrusa club, which was the Bermuda branch of a big American club organisation. They had meetings and outings and I met a number of very charming people and was invited to join the club committee. It was something quite different from anything else I had experienced as a QA.[7]

Margot had met many interesting people and had loved every minute of her post-war military career. Nursing had been her life and she had given all her enthusiasm, energy and dedication to preserving and guiding her profession. There were times, particularly during her retirement and her return journey to Muntok, when her mind wandered back to the Java Sea and the drifting makeshift raft – a time when the searing hot sun scorched her skin and parched her lips – and it was with an ever-increasing sense of wonderment that she viewed her incredulous survival.

Margot was not one to dwell on memories very much. She had always been a down-to-earth, straightforward person, who looked towards the future and tackled each problem in a quiet and dignified manner. When asked about her philosophy she maintained: 'I never think about myself much, I just think about what I have to do.'[8]

Following an eventful, interesting, purposeful and determined life of service, Dame Margot Evelyn Marguerite Turner died peacefully in Brighton on 24 September 1993. But to all the present-day members of the Queen Alexandra's Royal Army Nursing Corps her exemplary and shining example of courage, faith and leadership lives on, and continues to provide a source of endless inspiration to those who follow in her footsteps.

Notes

1. L. Warner & J. Sandilands, *Women Behind the Wire* (1982), pp. 1–2.
2. Imperial War Museum Oral History Interview with Dame Margot Turner, ref. 9126.
3. Ibid.

4. *Girls' Own* newspaper, November 1945, pp. 6–7, quoted by B. Tinkler, *Constructing Girlhood*, p. 114.

5. Mass Observation, *The Journey Home*, p. 117, quoted in P. Summerfield, *Reconstructing Women's Wartime Lives* (1998), p. 258.

6. IWM Oral History Interview with Dame Margot Turner, ref. 9126.

7. J. Smyth, *The Will to Live* (1970), p. 153.

8. Ibid. Also quoted on the official QARANC website.

Appendix

Second World War Timeline

1939

At outset of war, Margot is based with the Queen Alexandra's Royal Imperial Nursing Service in Bareilly, India.

July	**Margot posted to Ranikhet Hospital, India.**
31 August	The British government issues orders to evacuate forthwith. As a result, over 3.5 million men, women and children are evacuated from large urban cities to safer rural areas in preparation for war.
1 September	German forces invade Poland and Britain issues Germany with an ultimatum under the terms of the Anglo-Polish alliance.
3 September	Britain and France declare war on Germany.
17 September	Russian troops enter Poland. (Russia had signed a non-aggression pact with Germany, which was supposed to guarantee that Germany would not invade Russian territory.)

28 September	Poland is divided by Germany and Russia.
30 November	Russia invades Finland.
17 December	The last of the German 'pocket battleships', the *Graf Spee*, is scuttled at Montevideo on the orders of the German High Command. (This move was taken to avoid the embarrassing propaganda that would have ensued if the German population had found out that the ship had been severely damaged by the British Royal Navy during the Battle of the River Plate.)

1940

12 March	Peace treaty is signed between Russia and Finland.
9 April	German forces invade Denmark and Norway.
10 May	Germans invade Netherlands, Belgium and Luxembourg. Neville Chamberlain resigns and Winston Churchill takes his place as the British prime minister.
12 May	German forces cross the French border.
15 May	The Dutch army surrenders.
26 May–4 June	The Dunkirk evacuation of British troops, during which nearly 900 ships, some in private ownership, ferry 338,226 troops from Dunkirk back to Britain.
28 May	King Leopold surrenders Belgium.
10 June	Italy enters the war on the side of Germany.
14 June	German forces take over Paris.
15/16 June	Russian forces capture Lithuania, Latvia and Estonia.
22 June	France and Germany sign an armistice.
10 July	The Battle of Britain begins.
7 September	Start of the Blitz.
28 October	Italy invades Greece.

APPENDIX

1941

10 January	America introduces a lend-lease policy into Congress, which offers financial support to Britain's war effort.
1 March	**Margot reports to No 17 Combined General Hospital, Bombay.**
8 March	**Margot embarks for Singapore, where she is stationed at Tanjong Malim.**
30 March	German forces mount a counter-offensive in North Africa.
6 April	Germany invades Greece and Yugoslavia.
11 April	The Russians sign a neutrality treaty with Japan.
20 May	German forces invade Crete.
1 June	The British withdraw from Crete.
8 June	British and Free French forces enter Syria.
14 June	President Roosevelt freezes German and Italian funds in America.
22 June	Germany invades Russia, ending the terms of the non-aggression pact.
12 July	Britain and Russia sign a mutual aid pact.
14 August	The Atlantic Charter: Roosevelt and Churchill meet at sea to discuss war aims.
25 August	British and Russian troops enter Iran.
19 September	Germany captures Kiev.
11 October	General Tojo becomes Japan's premier.
18 November	The British Eighth Army begins a desert offensive in Libya.
28 November	Russian forces recapture Rostov.
1 December	The Russians stage a counter-offensive at Tula.
7 December	Japan attacks Pearl Harbor and destroys America's Pacific Fleet. Japan declares war on America and Britain.
8 December	Japanese forces land in Thailand and Malaya. America and Britain declare war on Japan.
9 December	Britain's HMS *Prince of Wales* and HMS *Repulse* are destroyed by Japanese aircraft off the coast of Malaya.

10/11 December	Germany and Italy declare war on America.
22 December	Japan begins a major offensive in the Philippines, and Churchill attends the first Washington Conference.
25 December	Hong Kong surrenders to the Japanese.

1942

1 January	The United Nations Declaration is signed by twenty-six nations. (The Declaration effectively provided an alliance which pledged the military and economic support of the signatories against Germany and Italy. The Declaration also formed the basis of the United Nations Organisation, which was established after hostilities had ceased.)
10/11 January	Japanese forces invade the Dutch East Indies.
21 January	German forces stage a counter-offensive in North Africa.
13 February	**Margot is evacuated from Singapore aboard *Kuala*.**
14 February	***Kuala* is bombed by the Japanese; the survivors swim to a nearby island.**
15 February	Singapore falls to the Japanese. The British are forced to surrender the island.
17 February	**Margot is rescued by the cargo ship *Tanjong Penang*, which is bombed the same day. Margot survives by tying two rafts together.**
21 February	**Margot is rescued by a Japanese destroyer and taken to Muntok harbour on the Dutch East Indies island of Banka.**
2 March	**Margot is interned in a Muntok prisoner-of-war camp.**
7 March	The evacuation of Rangoon.
17 March	The American General MacArthur arrives in Australia to discuss Allied war aims in the Far East.

1 April	**Margot is moved to Palembang.**
9 April	The American forces on Bataan surrender.
18 April	American aircraft launch bombing raids on Tokyo.
4–9 May	Battle of the Coral Sea.
26 May	Another German counter-offensive in North Africa.
30–31 May	The first Royal Air Force 'thousand bomber raid', under the command of Air Marshal Harris, takes place on Cologne.
4 June	Battle of Midway Island.
21 June	Germany captures Tobruk.
25–27 June	Second Washington Conference between Roosevelt and Churchill.
7 August	American forces land in Guadalcanal.
12 August	First Moscow Conference.
October	**Margot begins nursing Chinese and Malayan patients in Charitas Hospital.**
23 October	Montgomery strikes at El Alamein.
7/8 November	America and Britain undertake a massive reinforcement of their troops in North Africa.
19–22 November	The Russians stage a counter-offensive at Stalingrad.

1943

14–24 January	Casablanca Conference, attended by Churchill, Roosevelt and their chiefs of staff. Stalin did not attend as he was preoccupied with military campaigns near Stalingrad.
23 January	The British Eighth Army enters Tripoli.
2 February	The German force surrenders at Stalingrad.
2 March	Battle of the Bismarck Sea.
April	**Margot is arrested by the Kempeitai and thrown into Palembang prison.**
11–27 May	Third Washington Conference between Roosevelt and Churchill.

12 May	German and Italian resistance in Tunisia ends.
18 May	United Nations Food Conference takes place in Virginia.
5 July	Battle of Kursk begins. (The Russians eventually pushed back the Germans and were able to move onto the offensive along the whole of the Eastern Front. This battle signified a dramatic turning point in the war in Europe.)
9/10 July	British and American forces invade Sicily.
19 July	Bombing raids begin on Rome.
25 July	Mussolini is replaced by Badogolio as Italy's premier.
17–24 August	First Quebec Conference, attended by Churchill, Roosevelt and their chiefs of staff; Stalin declines to attend.
3 September	British and American forces invade Italy.
8 September	Italy surrenders.
9 September	British and American forces land at Salerno.
10 September	German forces occupy Rome.
October	**Margot is released from Palembang prison and returned to prisoner-of-war camp.**
13 October	Italy declares war on Germany.
6 November	The Russians recapture Kiev.
9 November	The United Nations Relief and Rehabilitation Administration is formed.
12 December	The Czecho-Russian alliance is formed.

1944

22 January	British and American forces land behind German lines at Anzio.
8 March	The Finns reject the terms of the Russian armistice.
19 March	German forces cross the Hungarian border.
April	**Margot's camp transferred from civil to military control. Commandant Siki now in charge.**

10 April	The Russians retake Odessa.
23 May	British and American troops launch an offensive from Anzio beachhead.
4 June	Rome is captured by British and American troops.
6 June	D-Day: British and American invasion of Normandy.
13/14 June	The first V-1 flying bombs (doodlebugs) land in Britain.
15 June	The first American B-29 Superfortress raid takes place on Japan.
3 July	The Russians recapture Minsk.
27 July	American troops break through west of St-Lo.
11 August	American forces occupy Guam.
15 August	British and American forces land on the French south coast.
25 August	Paris is liberated.
3 September	Brussels is liberated.
8 September	First V-2 rocket lands on London.
17 September	American and British troops land in Holland.
October	**Margot's camp is moved back to Muntok on Banka island.**
14 October	American and British forces occupy Athens.
20 October	Belgrade is liberated, and American troops invade the Philippines.
21/22 October	Battle of Leyte Gulf.
12 November	*Tirpitz* is sunk by the Royal Air Force.
16 December	The Germans launch their last major counter-offensive – Battle of the Bulge.

1945

9 January	American forces land on Lozon in the Philippines.
11 January	The Russians take Warsaw.
20 January	Hungary signs armistice.
27 January	Memel is liberated.

31 January	Churchill and Roosevelt meet at Malta.
3 February	American troops land at Manila.
4–12 February	Conference held at Yalta between Roosevelt, Stalin and Churchill.
19 February	American troops land on Iwo Jima.
7 March	The American First Army crosses the Rhine.
April	**All women prisoners of war are moved to Loebok Linggau, Sumatra.**
1 April	America invades Okinawa.
12 April	Roosevelt dies and is replaced by Truman as American president.
13 April	Vienna is liberated.
28 April	Mussolini is executed by partisan forces.
30 April	Hitler commits suicide in his bunker in Berlin; American forces liberate 33,000 inmates at Dachau concentration camp; and the Russian flag is raised on the Reichstag in Berlin.
1 May	Admiral Doenitz assumes command of Germany.
2 May	Berlin falls to the Russians.
3 May	Rangoon is captured.
7 May	Germany surrenders.
8 May	Victory in Europe Day.
17 July–2 August	Potsdam Conference, attended by Churchill, Truman and Stalin.
6 August	Atomic bomb is dropped on Hiroshima.
8 August	Russia declares war on Japan.
9 August	Second atomic bomb is dropped on Nagasaki.
14 August	Japan surrenders.
26 August	**Commandant Siki announces to the women prisoners that the war is over.**
2 September	Japan signs surrender terms in Tokyo Bay.
10 September	**Major Gideon Jacobs is parachuted into Margot's camp at Loebok Linggau to rescue the prisoners of war.**
18 September	**Margot leaves the camp for Singapore.**

Index